DUCHY ORIGINALS
COOKBOOK

DUCHY ORIGINALS
COOKBOOK

Johnny Acton and Nick Sandler

Foreword by His Royal Highness The Prince of Wales

PHOTOGRAPHY BY JONATHAN GREGSON

KYLE CATHIE LTD

Acknowledgements
We would like to thank everybody who works with Duchy Originals to produce their superb range of products and especially those who have given us their time for this book.

First published in Great Britain in 2006 by
Kyle Cathie Limited
122 Arlington Road, London NW1 7HP
general.enquiries@kyle-cathie.com
www.kylecathie.com

ISBN-13: 978 1 85626 653 6
ISBN-10: 1 85626 653 2

Text © 2006 Johnny Acton and Nick Sandler
Photographs © 2006 Jonathan Gregson
Book Design © 2006 by Kyle Cathie Limited
Duchy, Duchy Originals and the arms of the Duchy of Cornwall are the registered trade marks of Duchy Originals Limited.

Editorial Director: Muna Reyal
Designer: Carl Hodson
Photographer: Jonathan Gregson
Food Stylist: Linda Tubby
Props Stylist: Tabitha Hawkins
Assistant Editor: Georgina Atsiaris
Production: Sha Huxtable and Alice Holloway

Johnny Acton and Nick Sandler are hereby identified as the authors of this work in accordance with Section 77 of the Copyright, Designs and Patents Act 1988.

A Cataloguing in Publication record for this title is available from the British Library.

Colour reproduction by Chromagraphic
Printed in Singapore by Tien-Wah Press

Twenty years ago, I took the decision to establish an experiment at the Duchy Home Farm in Gloucestershire. Having long felt deeply about the widespread damage inflicted on the British landscape during the 1960s and 1970s, I was keen to do what I could to help reverse the harm.

I was particularly concerned by what we appeared to be discarding casually in the name of "progress", including rare breeds of livestock, time-honoured food production methods and any semblance of patience. In place of the prevailing attitude towards the natural world, I wanted to promote a sustainable approach to agriculture. It seemed clear that the way forward, for the sake of our descendants and the health of the soil, was to learn to work <u>with</u> Nature rather than against her. So, flying in the face of the conventional wisdom of the day, I decided it was time to convert to organic farming methods.

At the same time, not only was I becoming increasingly uneasy about the quality of the soulless, mass-produced food that had come to dominate the modern diet, but also about the long term future of farming in the UK. I felt that it was vital to create marketing initiatives that added value to agricultural produce. In 1990, I therefore commissioned some research into the feasibility of a small range of agricultural marketing initiatives. The idea of a food brand was presented; a brand which would endorse high quality products made with the best ingredients, expertly produced in harmony with the environment. Thus Duchy Originals was conceived. In 1992 the first product was launched: an oaten biscuit made from wheat and oats grown at Home Farm. Inevitably, we had some early teething problems, but I am delighted to say that the 'experiment' has proved a great success. Today Duchy Originals has more than 200 products, all made in the UK in partnership with some of the country's best food manufacturers.

It is in the context of the ongoing effort to publicize the benefits of sustainable and organic agriculture that I particularly welcome the *Duchy Originals Cookbook*. For a long time I have felt that the fundamental problem with the food culture in this country has been the historical severance of the link between the consumer and the land, and I hope that the food industry will strive to heal the split. I am convinced that with even better marketing, and greater transparency and traceability, we will be able to reconnect the consumer with the farmer and the producer and so rebuild a thriving, indigenous food culture in this country.

I hope that the *Duchy Originals Cookbook* will inspire many more people to care about what they eat and where it comes from and, above all, to enjoy and benefit from eating it.

The History of Duchy Originals

If you're out shopping for food in the UK and you come across a tempting, organic item in smart packaging, there is a good chance that it's a Duchy Original.

Duchy Originals is a paradox, an increasingly high-profile brand that champions quality, supports ethical initiatives and seeks to offer an alternative to mass-market culture. You can buy Duchy food in the supermarket and it is tailored to suit modern tastes, yet it has all the old-fashioned virtues. It is made in a traditional, unhurried manner, is not bulked up with water and there are no chemical additives. The ingredients have been grown and raised in harmony with Nature, and the results taste the opposite of plastic.

Duchy Originals was founded by HRH The Prince of Wales in 1990. The aim was to promote the wider adoption of organic farming and food production methods in order to benefit the wider environment, to demonstrate the importance of adding value and better marketing and to assist the smaller family farmer to meet increasing challenges through co-operative ventures. As he has written in his foreword, Prince Charles had long been concerned about the prevailing food culture in Britain and its environmental and social impact. He was already putting his ideas into practice on the Duchy of Cornwall Home Farm in Gloucestershire, which had been gradually converting to the organic system over the preceding six years. Following on from this he wanted to encourage others to do the same. This meant proving that the approach was economically viable and that the public would want to eat the results.

To this end, it was decided to set up a food brand. The idea was to establish a kind of alternative seal of excellence, a label guaranteeing that the contents were top quality, British made, and produced in accordance with the principles of sustainability. It also needed a name easily recognisable to the public. After some deliberation, 'Duchy Originals' was chosen. The first part of the name was taken from the Duchy of Cornwall estates, which are held in trust by the Prince, who is also the Duke of Cornwall. The 'Originals' was designed to emphasise the uniqueness of the brand, and its aspiration to create truly original premium-quality food.

The venture needed to be profitable, and not only because this is legally required of the business activities of the Duchy of Cornwall estates. As the Prince has said, 'I wanted to demonstrate that it was possible to produce food of the highest quality, working in harmony with the environment and Nature, using the best ingredients and adding value through expert production.' There was also another incentive for Duchy Originals: profits were to go to The Prince's Charities Foundation. As one of the functions of the Foundation is to fund agricultural and environmental initiatives, if everything went to plan, a 'virtuous circle' would be established. Duchy Originals would

encourage others to go organic, both indirectly, by serving as a positive example, and directly, by reinvesting the profits in relevant charities. The public, meanwhile, would learn just how excellent sustainably produced food can be and have the comfort of knowing that its purchases were contributing to good causes.

The first Duchy Originals product was an oaten biscuit, made with oats and wheat harvested at Duchy Home Farm and then stone-ground at the local Shipton Mill. To develop the biscuit, the help of one of the finest bakers in the UK was enlisted: Walkers Shortbread Ltd of Aberlour in the Scottish Highlands. It took 18 months and almost 200 sample batches to fine tune the recipe, but in 1992 the biscuit was launched, and to great acclaim. It was declared 'the ideal accompaniment to cheese and sweet spreads'.

The successful relationship with Walkers set the pattern for the future. Duchy Originals has built up its range through close working partnerships with a selection of small- to medium-sized farms and businesses. All have established reputations for commitment to quality. We will meet many of the remarkable men and women involved in the course of this book, characters like Paul Kelly in Essex, proud pioneer of the KellyBronze Turkey, and Freddie de Lisle, who is resurrecting the original stilton cheese at Quenby Hall in Leicestershire.

Duchy Home Farm remains a key supplier for many Duchy Originals products. In addition to the organic grain used for the biscuits, the farm is the source of pork for the delicatessen ham, sausages and bacon, which were added to the range in 1997, also an old variety of barley called Plumage Archer for ale, root vegetables for crisps and chutneys, mustard seed for wholegrain mustard, and, since 2001, milk from the Ayrshire herd. Meanwhile, Duchy Selections heather honey is harvested on royal land adjacent to Balmoral in Aberdeenshire.

The Duchy Originals experiment can be declared an unqualified success. When Prince Charles and his farm manager David Wilson began the conversion of Duchy Home Farm in 1986, they had no way of knowing that an organic explosion lay around the corner, but their instincts have proved well founded. Annual sales of organic food have topped £1 billion in the United Kingdom and are predicted to grow by more than £2 million a week. Duchy Originals itself has gone from strength to strength. The oaten biscuit has been joined by over 200 quintessentially British products and turnover has climbed to £56 million. In 1999 the company moved into profit for the first time, and to date some £6 million has been raised for The Prince of Wales's Charities Foundation.

The Duchy Philosophy

Since its inception, Duchy Originals has been guided by a clear philosophy. The brand has six interrelated goals:

TO PROMOTE SUSTAINABLE AND WHEREVER POSSIBLE ORGANIC AGRICULTURE

All products with the Duchy Originals label are thoroughly organic. As the brand has evolved, it has sought to extend its support of sustainability into other areas. A case in point is wild fish. Duchy Originals works closely with the Marine Stewardship Council (MSC) to ensure that the mackerel and herring used in its patés are sourced from sustainable fisheries (see pages 141–145), but they cannot be classified as organic as it is impossible to know the feeding history of the main ingredients. Similarly, the Balmoral honey (see pages 89–92) isn't organic, largely because of the difficulty of proving where the bees have harvested their pollen as they can fly several miles and partly because all the existing colonies would have had to be replaced for the beekeeper to earn an organic certificate. A sister label called 'Duchy Selections' has been set up to denote foods farmed or harvested in a sustainable but not strictly organic fashion.

TO MAKE 'REAL' FOOD, USING TRADITIONAL, PATIENT METHODS COMBINED WITH CONTEMPORARY CULINARY CREATIVITY

The Duchy Originals suppliers are repositories of traditional know-how, but they are also innovators. You only have to witness the computerised milking system at the Home Farm Dairy (see pages 51–52) to realise that the company is more than happy to embrace technology where it works harmoniously with Nature, but change is never adopted for its own sake. The Duchy Originals enterprise is underpinned by timeless values like patience, quality and taste. There is no resort to shortcuts and everything is conducted on a human scale. As long as they produce the best results, time-honoured methods are always used in preference to modern alternatives. (They usually do, which is why they are time honoured.) The preserves, for example, are boiled in traditional copper pans (see pages 107–108). Duchy Originals is also a champion of rare breeds and neglected plant strains.

The company may promote traditional values and practices, but there is nothing fusty about Duchy Originals food, as this book aims to

illustrate. Quality never goes out of fashion – indeed the reverse is true according to recent trends – and the company is acutely aware of the needs and tastes of the discerning modern customer.

TO SHOWCASE THE BEST BRITISH PRODUCE

All Duchy Originals ingredients are sourced from Britain, except where this is impossible for reasons of quality or climate, in which case they are obtained from organic farms abroad. The Seville marmalade, for example, is made with Spanish oranges and the cocoa for the chocolate comes from organic co-operatives in Commonwealth countries such as Guyana.

TO WORK IN HARMONY WITH NATURE, FOLLOWING THE RHYTHM OF THE SEASONS

Respect for the natural world comes automatically with the organic territory. The Prince of Wales is an advocate of seasonal food and would avoid serving asparagus in November. The authors agree.

TO RECONNECT PEOPLE WITH THE FOOD ON THEIR PLATES

Duchy Originals was set up to offer an alternative to anonymous, mass-produced food, and to help reverse the historical split between farmers and

the public. The company strives to have strong stories behind all its offerings, to give back food its human or animal face and reassure consumers about its provenance. This book can be seen as a contribution to the process.

TO DONATE PROFITS TO THE PRINCE'S CHARITIES FOUNDATION, AND THEREBY TO PROMOTE SUSTAINABLE AGRICULTURE FURTHER

Ideally – and in reality, to judge by the growth of Duchy Originals – each of these ambitions reinforces the others in a virtuous circle. The more good organic food becomes available, the more people want to eat it, which encourages more people to produce it and so on. The result is a better diet, a better environment and a better future.

The Cookbook

This book has two simple premises: it matters where our food comes from and it matters what we do with it.

Duchy Originals and like-minded companies are already addressing the first premise, by producing top-quality organic food and getting it on the shelves of our shops, but what about the second question? Once we have all these wonderful ingredients, what are we going to make with them? After all, the journey that begins in the fields ends up in our mouths.

The *Duchy Originals Cookbook* aims to tackle both sides of the equation. First, we show you exactly where Duchy food comes from. We visit the places it is grown, reared, caught, harvested and processed and meet the people responsible. Then we provide some inspiring suggestions for getting the most out of it. Some of the 100-odd recipes are our own, others come from Duchy suppliers, the people who know and love the ingredients best.

We were desperate to write this book, not because we work for Duchy Originals (we don't), but because we agree so thoroughly with what the company is trying to do. Our angle of approach is unashamedly culinary – probably just as well given that we're writing a cookbook – and we speak primarily from the stomach. We could, though, just as easily be writing from our consciences. The beauty of top-quality organic food is that it's extremely enjoyable to eat, yet you're doing the 'right thing' when you eat it. It is a win-win situation, for your taste buds, your body, the environment and, where applicable, the animals who are feeding you. To buy Duchy ingredients, or other food made in the same spirit, is a form of enlightened self-interest.

The one thing that people fear organic food may harm is their bank balance. There is no way round the fact that organic produce is often more expensive than the factory-farmed equivalent, but replace the word 'organic' with 'good' and the first half of this sentence still holds true. In the end, it is a matter of priorities. Since 1970, the proportion of the average household income spent on food has fallen from 25 per cent to little more than 10. There is clearly some slack if we choose to use it. We believe food is too important to be relegated to a cost-cutting exercise.

Frankly, the food culture that has been dominant in the UK until recently has made a visit to the average farm or processing unit – where there is still a distinction – a fairly depressing experience. Having spent 12 months immersing ourselves in the world of Duchy Originals, though, the word that suggests itself is 'uplifting'. The fields are clean and fragrant, the animals manifestly enjoy their lives and the suppliers come across as fulfilled people, proud of what they do. This book is a celebration of their work. We hope it is a glowing endorsement not only of Duchy Originals, but equally if not more importantly the Duchy way of thinking.

NAVIGATION

The structure of the *Duchy Originals Cookbook* is determined by the seasons, in line with the philosophy of working and eating in harmony with Nature. Beginning in Spring, we follow the company through one annual cycle. Each chapter has three elements: a seasonal overview in which we give a summary of 'what's going down on the farm', features in which we zoom in on particular foods, processes and personalities, and of course, the recipes themselves. Some of these are traditional favourites; others are thoroughly contemporary.

Most of the recipes and features pop up where you might expect. The majority of Duchy products are inherently seasonal, either because their raw materials mature at specific times of the year (fruits, grains and vegetables) or because they are traditionally eaten at particular festivals: chocolate eggs at Easter, goose at Christmas. This makes it pretty obvious where to place them in the book. Warming stews appear in the Winter chapter and salads in the Summer. Some of the foods we look at, however, notably dairy products and bacon, are produced year round. We have tried to deal with non-seasonal foods intuitively and with an eye on the balance of the book, but if you're looking for something specific, there's always the index and table of contents!

INTELLIGENT SHOPPING

Although Duchy Originals and similar companies are making it easier to buy top-quality ingredients, shopping for the best requires your active participation. We advise you to buy organic and sustainably farmed foods for the simple reason that they invariably make better eating than the alternatives, but this isn't quite the end of the story. For one thing, companies like Duchy Originals don't produce all the ingredients you are likely to need. Fresh organic vegetables, for example, you will probably have to source yourself. For another, although organic is good, not all organic food is as good as it might be. Some organic products are made with love and craft; others are skimped in a rush to join the bandwagon. The fact that a food bears an organic label doesn't mean that it is necessarily in peak condition. You need to shop with your eyes open.

In this book, we encourage you to do two things. First, talk to people. Go to farmers' markets and chat to the stallholders. Get to know your local butcher, fishmonger and greengrocer and ask them questions. Where do they source their products? How are they reared or grown? What is particularly good at the moment? Do they have any tips for cooking or accompaniments? Your curiosity will be handsomely rewarded.

The second key to eating in line with the Duchy Originals philosophy is to think seasonally. This will ensure that you catch ingredients at their best. You will also find yourself eagerly anticipating seasonal specialities that you once took for granted. As soon as you give up taking the line of least resistance, namely buying the product nearest to you on the shelf, regardless of provenance or seasonality, your food life will become infinitely more rewarding. You feel more like a twenty-first century hunter-gatherer and less like a passive consumer. In the absence, for example, of fresh tomatoes in Winter, you are forced to think a little more creatively. This can only benefit your cooking. Eating becomes an adventure again.

SPRING

Spring is all about new life, wherever you happen to be, but in the fields and farmyards of the Duchy Originals world, things somehow feel 'springier' to your authors. The emerging greens seem greener in an organic environment, the smells more vivid and the livestock more skittish. Nature is waking up. Animals which were cooped up in the Winter joyfully take advantage of the liberty the change of season brings, the pigs catching every available ray of sun, the cattle feasting on sweet new grass and clover. Meanwhile crop planting is high on the agenda.

In this chapter, we drop in on several Duchy suppliers at one of the busiest times of year. The accent in Spring is on preparation and growth. Relatively few Duchy Originals products reach maturity at this time of year, although we do take an in-depth look at lamb here, which is raised at Home Farm independently of the company. Nevertheless, there is plenty of activity behind the scenes. This is breeding time, for instance, for the KellyBronze turkeys. The offspring won't be ready for the table for several months, but here we take a look at them at the beginning of their lives. We will meet them again in the Winter chapter.

This is also where we first encounter the Duchy pigs. The piglets are born throughout the year, but because Spring is associated with birth, it seems particularly appropriate to feature them here. We also visit the Prince's woodland in Herefordshire, where the wood for smoking the Duchy ham and smoked salmon is sourced. Ninety-five per cent of the woodland owned by the Duchy of Cornwall is certified as sustainable by the Forestry Stewardship Council, and here we find out what this entails. We also show how sustainable forestry fits into the holistic Duchy Originals vision.

We begin, however, with a tour of Home Farm, the template for Duchy Originals and the birthplace of the brand.

HOME FARM

'it's all in the soil!'

Home Farm is situated amid the gently rolling countryside of southern Gloucestershire in the South West of England. When the Prince of Wales purchased Highgrove in the 1980s, the estate had a mere 25 acres of farmland. The figure has since risen to 1,900: 1,100 acres at Home Farm and 800 share-farmed with neighbours.

The first thing to strike the visitor to Home Farm is how neat and orderly everything is. There are no piles of rusting machinery and the farm buildings and fences are immaculately maintained. There is also a deep sense of peace.

We park up, and are greeted by David Wilson, the farm manager. Wilson is a tall, lean, enthusiastic man of about fifty. He has managed Home Farm since 1985, and has therefore presided over the whole of the organic conversion process. At his initial interview for the post, he had the wit to say that he was interested in organic farming, but by his own admission this interest was largely theoretical. He has had to learn on the job. Wilson's pride in what has been achieved at Home Farm is palpable, but he isn't entirely immune to the anxiety that seems to be an occupational hazard. Whether it's a ewe with a damaged leg or the weather forecast, there is always something to worry about. A farmer's work is never done.

The purpose of our trip is to get the overall lie of the land and an insight into the workings of the organic system. David summarises this in five words. 'It's all in the soil', he explains. We then clamber into his rather battered Land Rover so he can show us directly how he goes about ensuring the fertility and continued health of this fundamental commodity.

Clockwise from top left Nairobi carrots used in the Duchy Originals Vegetable Crisps. Clover silage for the cows. Potato plants at Home Farm. A poppy growing in the oat fields – a healthy sign of biodiversity. David Wilson, Home Farm Manager. Nitrogen-fixing fabia field beans (Maris Bead variety).

The organic system employed at Home Farm revolves around a seven-year cycle of crop rotation. For the first three years, any given field will be given over to clover and grass. This provides nutritious grazing for the farm's animals, who return the favour in the form of manure, thereby replenishing the soil. In year four, Winter wheat is grown. At Home Farm, an old variety called Maris Widgeon is planted. It produces long, fast-growing stalks which outpace weeds, removing the need for chemical herbicides. The following year, the field is planted with oats. In year six, fabia beans are grown, which provide fodder for cattle and replenish the soil with nitrogen, of which wheat and oats are hungry consumers. Then, in the final year of the cycle, the field is used to grow either rye or Spring barley. Meanwhile, in each of years four to seven, turnips, which are also nitrogen fixing, are grown in the 'windows' between crops. They also provide a useful supplement for the livestock.

As we trundle around Home Farm and its outlying fields, we begin to get a picture of how everything fits together. For now, much of the action is beneath the soil, but we will be returning to the farm several times to look at the crops and livestock in greater depth and monitor their progress.

LAMBS

At the time of writing Duchy Originals is only marketing one lamb product, an excellent ready-made stew made with organic lamb and pearl barley, but the Duchy philosophy applies to sheep too. They are an important part of both the diet and the traditional rural economy in Britain, and nowhere is their historical influence more apparent than in Gloucestershire. The area around Highgrove grew rich on the medieval wool trade.

There are 430 breeding ewes on Home Farm. One freezing Spring morning, we meet Ken Foster the stockman (pictured on the opposite page) to see how the lambing season is progressing. Ken is a short, funny and direct man, probably in his late thirties, with a West Shropshire accent so thick it's almost Welsh. He has been working with sheep since he was nine and exudes confidence in what he does.

The weather is unfit for human consumption, so it is a relief to find that the animals are currently indoors. Ken organises the breeding to ensure that the lambs at Home Farm are born in two waves: one in March and one in April. The grass only really starts growing in April, particularly in cold years, so the first generation spends its first few weeks indoors. Only the April lambs are born in the fields.

The March lambs and their mothers are housed in three barns. They are divided into groups of two or three nursing ewes plus young, each group having a straw-filled pen to itself. We lean on the gate of a particularly photogenic pen, and ask Ken questions about the flock. Most of the sheep on the farm, he tells us, are Lleyns, the breed taking its name from the Welsh peninsula from which it originates. The Lleyn

is a prolific breed, which produces lots of milk and hardy lambs. The wool is only so-so, but the meat is excellent. The lambs put on weight quickly, but not excessively: Lleyn meat is usually graded two or three out of five on the industry fatness scale, which is ideal. Most of it goes to Fortnum & Mason or The Ritz in London. Ken also breeds a few faster-maturing lambs to supply a couple of speciality butcher clients with meat early in the season. They are produced by putting a Hampshire Down ram onto a Lleyn ewe, and are plumper than their pure-bred cousins, with a fat rating of four.

Lleyns are elegant, intelligent-looking sheep, and the two-week-old lambs are extremely cute. In their snow-white fleeces, they conform closely to one's mental image of Mary's pet in the nursery rhyme. One lamb takes the analogy a little too far for Ken's liking. It has to be bottle fed, having been rejected by its mother, and as a consequence has taken to following him around everywhere he goes. This may sound sweet to outsiders, but it irritates Ken, who has several hundred other sheep to look after. The lamb will also be difficult to sell: it can no longer be classified as organic because it survives on inorganic milk powder, the only kind currently available.

As we chat away, a curious ewe walks over and nuzzles Johnny's hand. Like most of her sisters, she has twins, but triplets are also common, and singletons slightly less so. Ewes only have two teats, so the policy is to pass a 'spare' triplet onto all the mothers with just one lamb. This is done, Ken explains, by smearing the incoming lamb with the singleton's afterbirth. All being well, she will assume it belongs to her and adopt it. He also has a technique to get rejected lambs adopted, but it depends on the death of another lamb, which is a rare occurrence on Home Farm. When a ewe does lose a lamb, Ken skins it and places the fleece over a suitable foundling. All being well, the bereaved ewe will recognise the scent and suckle the newcomer. Unfortunately, no suitable surrogate mother was available for the bottle-fed lamb we met earlier. Ken is known for his skill in this operation. One day he showed a lamb cunningly disguised in another's fleece to some members of the local constabulary. Apparently they still gossip about the miraculous two-tailed animal in Tetbury police station.

The majority of the Home Farm lambs are slaughtered at ten to twelve weeks, by which time they weigh 20-22kg (44-48lb). Some,

however, are kept on to provide the next generation of breeding ewes. To identify the best candidates, Ken weighs the lambs at birth, eight weeks and, where applicable, 22 weeks. He also raises a few pure-bred Hebrideans for the small but growing market for mutton, of which Prince Charles is a great proponent. These animals are sold to high-class butchers at twelve months. This is the optimum age for taste according to Ken, but the meat is necessarily expensive and exclusive due to the high cost of nurturing the sheep for a year.

It is farm policy to keep a few representatives of rare and endangered breeds, and before we leave, Ken draws our attention to a spectacularly dreadlocked Ryland ewe. He then introduces us to his border collies. There are two working dogs, Pippa and Spot, plus ten-year-old Ben who has retired due to arthritis. They bark ferociously as we return to the car, but wouldn't hurt a fly.

When we return to Home Farm a few months later, we see exactly how sheep fit into the farm's organic system. For those accustomed to seeing sheep grazing in exposed landscapes, it comes as a novelty to find them hidden in waist-high vegetation, but this is where we discover them. They are clearly very happy with their circumstances and are gorging themselves on clover. The plant simultaneously feeds the animals and returns nutrients to the soil (clover is leguminous), and the sheep fertilise the soil with their droppings. It is all very neat.

Clockwise from left Retired sheepdog Ben, with Ken. Sheepdog Pippa in action. This lamb was rejected by her mother and is bottle fed instead. Feeding the ewes. Mother and lamb.

Home Farm Lamb Stew

Serves 4 • This simple, warming stew is an excellent way to utilise some of the leftover lamb stock from the pasty recipe on page 26. The pearl barley gives it a Scotch broth-like quality.

a dab of olive oil

400g (14oz) diced lamb

a large pat of butter

2 sticks of celery, roughly sliced

1 medium leek, roughly sliced

2 medium carrots, peeled and roughly sliced

400ml (14fl oz) lamb stock (see recipe on page 205)

fresh rosemary and a bay leaf

100g (3½oz) dry weight pearl barley, cooked according to packet instructions

salt and pepper

Splash a little olive oil into a large saucepan and fry the lamb over moderate to fierce heat for a few minutes until nicely browned
Turn the heat down to moderate and add the butter.
Add the celery, leek and carrots and fry for 10-15 minutes, stirring occasionally.
Add the lamb stock plus the rosemary and bay leaf. Simmer for 1½ hours, topping up with lamb stock (or water) if necessary.
Add the cooked pearl barley and season with salt and pepper. Serve with slices of crusty bread and buttered Savoy cabbage.

Barbecued Lamb

Serves 6–8 • There is something atavistically satisfying about a barbecued leg of lamb. The aroma as it cooks will help you understand why the God of the Old Testament allowed Abraham to substitute a burnt offering of ram for his son Isaac. Only in this case the last thing you want is to burn your precious meat, so make sure the barbecue isn't too hot.

Use a 2kg (4lb 8oz) leg of lamb for this recipe. Ask your butcher to bone it out. This will leave you with one flat piece of meat weighing about 1.3kg (3lb). Take a sharp knife and score the lamb criss-cross fashion on each side to help the marinade penetrate.

2kg (4lb 8oz) leg of lamb, boned

THE MARINADE

juice of 1 lemon

4 garlic cloves, chopped

1 tablespoon roughly chopped fresh thyme

1 tablespoon roughly chopped fresh sage leaves

1 tablespoon dried marjoram

a good scattering of Maldon sea salt

plenty of pepper

1 tablespoon olive oil

¼ bottle Duchy Originals ale

Mix all the ingredients and steep the lamb in the marinade for at least a couple of hours.
Lay the meat flat onto the barbecue, placing the shelf at a height that translates to moderate heat. Cook for 20-25 minutes, depending on whether you like your lamb rare or medium.
Allow the lamb to rest for a good 10-15 minutes before you eat it. This will even out the internal temperature and help tenderise the meat.
Serve the barbecued lamb with a herb salad (see page 81) and some Duchy Originals tomato chutney on the side.

Lamb and Madeira Cornish Pasties

Serves 4 • Pasties have been a Cornish speciality for centuries. The thick pastry crimping was developed as a disposable 'handle' for tin miners, whose hands were liable to be contaminated with arsenic. Madeira, though, can rarely have featured as an ingredient unless the baker knew an accommodating smuggler.

THE STOCK

see the recipe for lamb stock on page 205

THE PASTRY

see the Old English pastry recipe on page 204

THE FILLING

a drop of olive oil

400g (14oz) diced lamb

a small piece of butter

1 small leek, washed and roughly chopped

2 medium carrots, peeled and roughly chopped

100ml (3½fl oz) dry or sweet Madeira

2 level tablespoons plain flour

1 teaspoon chopped fresh thyme

300g (10½oz) potato, roughly diced

lightly whisked egg for the glaze

salt and freshly ground pepper

Make the lamb stock, following the recipe on page 205. Note that it needs at least 3, preferably 5 hours, cooking time.

Make the pastry, following the Old English pastry recipe on page 204.

Heat a little olive oil in a pan, then fry the lamb for a few minutes over moderate heat until nicely browned.

Add the butter, leek and carrots and continue to fry for another 5 minutes, stirring frequently.

Add the Madeira and reduce by half over moderate heat. Stir in the flour.

Heat the lamb stock and slowly add it, stirring constantly. Add the thyme and potato. Simmer for 20 minutes, season, then allow the mixture to cool.

You are now ready to construct the pasties. Preheat the oven to 230ºC/450ºF/gas mark 8 and have a lightly whisked egg to hand. Remove the dough from the fridge and divide into 4 equal balls. Then take each of your dough balls and roll them into quite thin rounds. Place a line of meat filling across the centre of each, then dampen the sides with a little water and pull them up so they meet in the middle above the meat. Squeeze the sides together and crimp with your thumb and index finger. Then place the pasties on a greased baking sheet, brush them with egg, and bake for 10 minutes.

Finally, turn the heat down to 180ºC/350ºF/gas mark 4 and cook for another 40 minutes, checking the pasties from time to time and reducing the heat slightly if they seem to be cooking too fast.

Stuffed Leg of Mutton

Serves 6 • We have a well-thumbed copy of Mrs Beeton's classic nineteenth-century cookery book, and it sometimes feels as if half of it is devoted to mutton. Prior to World War II, few people in this country even considered eating lamb less than a year old, due to its relative lack of flavour. Mutton has a deeper, more robust taste and is not necessarily tougher, particularly if it is properly cooked, i.e. slowly and for a long time.

There are many specialist suppliers now selling mutton, including Craig Farm Organics, Sheepdrove and North Ronaldsay Mutton. In early 2006, the renaissance was confirmed by a sumptuous dinner at The Ritz, hosted by the Prince of Wales.

If you are unfamiliar with mutton and its preparation, this traditionally spiced recipe is an excellent starting point.

1 small leg of mutton (about 3kg/6lb 10oz), boned

olive oil, for rubbing

500ml (18fl oz) chicken or lamb stock

100ml (3½fl oz) dry or sweet Madeira

THE STUFFING

50g (2oz) Duchy Originals streaky bacon, roughly chopped

4 tablespoons freshly made breadcrumbs

1 medium onion, chopped

a sprig or 2 of parsley, chopped

8 sage leaves, chopped

2 teaspoons chopped thyme

1 teaspoon lemon zest

¼ freshly grated nutmeg

100g (3½oz) minced pork or lamb

salt and freshly ground pepper

Preheat the oven to 220ºC/425ºF/gas mark 7.

Mix together the bacon, breadcrumbs, onion, parsley, sage, thyme, lemon zest, nutmeg and minced pork or lamb in a large bowl with a little salt and pepper.

Stuff the leg of mutton with the above mixture via the aperture left by the departed bone, and secure the opening with string or skewer. Season the joint with salt and pepper and rub with olive oil.

Roast for 30 minutes, then turn the heat down to 180ºC/350ºF/ gas mark 4 and continue to cook for another 2 hours.

Remove the leg of mutton from the roasting dish and allow it to rest for about 15-20 minutes. In the meantime, pour the chicken or lamb stock and Madeira into the dish and reduce by half over moderate heat to make a jus.

Carve the mutton and serve with the jus, cabbage and roasted root vegetables.

PIGS

Scrubbet's Farm is not far from Home Farm, but stands at a higher elevation and feels more exposed. On the day of our visit, the sky is leaden, and Richard Hazel is worried because high winds are forecast. Pigs don't like wind.

Richard is a large, wry man in charge of some 3,000 swine. The animals are divided into three groups: two breeding units and a 'finishing' unit, to which the young pigs are transferred when they reach 12 to 14 weeks. The 'standard' Duchy pig contains genes from three breeds: Duroc (50 per cent), Large White and Landrace (25 per cent each). In other words, one of its parents will be a Duroc and the other a Landrace/Large White cross. The Duroc is a brown pig with a high fat content; the other breeds are pink, the Landrace with floppy ears and the Large White with pert ones. Pure representatives of each breed are kept at the main farm to produce the requisite bloodlines. They enjoy their reproductive work: there is no recourse to artificial insemination.

The result is a pleasing animal which may or may not be covered in attractive coloured splodges. It has a higher fat content than most commercial pigs because of its Duroc ancestry. As a result, it is hardier and better tasting than average, but less profitable per pound. Duchy Originals are happy to bear the cost: the goal, as always, is quality.

Before he became a Duchy tenant, Richard farmed pigs outdoors but not organically. He explains the differences over a cup of tea. To begin with, the animals have more space. An organic piggery covers two to three times the acreage of a conventional farm, and the pigs are moved to clean pasture more frequently. This guarantees them fresh rooting opportunities and minimises the chances of parasite infestation. Although the pigs are vaccinated – the risk of unnecessary suffering would be unacceptable if they were not – there is no prophylactic (pre-emptive) use of antibiotics.

Thus briefed, we make our way to the breeding unit in the field next to Richard's house. It is always interesting to see a proverbial situation actually happening, as when you round the corner of a country road to find a chicken ambling across without apparent reason. A pig in clover, on the evidence of our visit to Scrubbet's Farm, is every bit as happy as the expression would suggest.

Pigs are enthusiasts. The breeding unit, as we approach, is a scene of high animation, and at first we assume something special must be going on, but it's just pigs being pigs. They are fascinated by their environment and each other, and are constantly rooting, scratching, grunting or all three. They also have a complex social system which is reflected in their housing arrangements. For the first four weeks, the piglets live with their mothers in dedicated farrowing huts, and there may be as many as sixteen in a litter. They are then moved to larger, multi-family houses, where they are encouraged to suckle other sows for the beneficial effect on their antibodies. The only relatively solitary pigs are the boars. They live in fenced-off areas, but have the consolation of a fresh pair of sows every fortnight.

After spending an enjoyable half-hour watching the pigs go about their business, we make our way to the 'finishing unit'. The animals are transferred here at 12–14 weeks, and remain until they are ready for the abattoir at about five and a half months. The object of the exercise is to fatten them up: they will weigh over 100kg (220lb) by the time they are slaughtered. The adolescent pigs are particularly mischievous. We are advised to stay clear of one pen because the inhabitants are 'rogering everything that moves'. One of the neighbours nips the photographer on the bottom. Richard

rhapsodises about their cleverness. He has known pigs to make their own wallows by overturning troughs or chewing through water-pipes when their existing ones run dry.

Our final port of call is a second breeding unit, located on land belonging to the Royal Agricultural College. Here, we have the charming experience of holding day-old piglets. We also peer into a hut where a sow has just given birth. Watching her suckling her young is profoundly soothing.

There is inevitably something heartbreaking about knowing that these delightful animals are going to be killed for the table, and one gets the distinct impression that Richard feels the same, beneath a layer of professional hardness. But any regret is tempered by three realisations. First, this is the pigs' raison d'être. They are domesticated animals, unlikely to do well in the wild, and if they hadn't been tamed, their ancestors would long ago have been hunted to extinction (at least in the UK; there are admittedly a few wild boar left in less populated parts of the world). Second, if we're going to eat bacon and pork, we definitely want it to come from animals that have lived like these ones. Finally, if we were domestic pigs, we'd want to live like them too.

BACON

Since 1999, the Duchy Originals bacon has been cured by Denhay Farms Ltd in Dorset. The main farm is situated in Marshwood Vale, a few miles inland from Lyme Bay, in a designated Area of Outstanding Natural Beauty. The surroundings are genuinely idyllic, and the climate is dry and mild by British standards, which is a big advantage when curing pork products. The weather is certainly fantastic on the day of our visit.

We are greeted by George Streatfeild, the Managing Director, and his wife Amanda, who is in charge of marketing. The Streatfeild family have been running the operation since 1952, when George's father, known as 'the Commander', joined forces with Lord Hood to incorporate the company.

George and Amanda correctly calculate that the best way to show us what they do is to feed us. Accordingly, they give us a fantastic lunch on the farmhouse patio. We sit beneath a heavily vined trellis, drink in the view, and settle down to a meal of Denhay produce. In addition to the Duchy range, the company produces its own brand

hams and bacons, an English air-dried prosciutto, and West Country cheddar made with milk from the farm's five cattle herds. The Streatfeilds also make their own butter. Throw in some home-grown organic vegetables and crusty brown rolls and you couldn't have a simpler or more excellent meal.

While we are eating, there is a scrabbling overhead, and a kitten emerges from the overhead vines. 'That'll be Paws', says Amanda. Paws has six toes on each foot, rather than the regulation four. Apparently cats with this unusual characteristic are relatively common in this area. They are sometimes known as Hemingway cats, after the famous author, who used to keep a few. The extra toes are no problem for the enchanting little animal; if anything, they help it negotiate the trellis-work.

Although George waxes lyrical about the farm's production methods – he is particularly excited by a new 'smokeless' smoker which works by friction, thus reducing tarry deposits in the meat – we don't actually get to see any ham or bacon being cured. George candidly explains why: the curing unit will shortly be moving to Honiton in Devon, and so is in relative disarray at the moment. He also doesn't want anyone, let alone a pair of foodies, to discover how he makes Denhay air-dried ham. Many have tried and many have failed to produce a quality English prosciutto, but George and his team have cracked it. The air-dried ham is the company's USP ('unique selling proposition'), and its secrets are jealously guarded.

Instead of a tour of the curing unit, George talks us through the process in great detail (see sidebar opposite). He goes on to outline the characteristics to look for in top-notch bacon. As he does so, Amanda dishes up some prime examples in the form of several rashers of Duchy Originals streaky bacon. They have simply been cooked in an Aga for 10 minutes and are quite delicious. There is a notable absence of white goo, that familiar but unwelcome by-product of lesser bacon that has been bulked up with water. This meat is succulent and not too salty, and the superior quality of the fat is unmistakable. Because of the low water content, it has crisped up nicely rather than boiled in its own liquid.

As we depart, the Streatfeilds' daughter pulls up. It turns out that she is working for Hugh Fearnley-Whittingstall, another champion of good meat, a mile or two down the road.

Right Pig farmer, Richard Hazel.

BACON À LA DUCHY

The Duchy Originals organic bacon is cured simply and traditionally. First it is rubbed with sea salt, a little organic sugar and a tiny amount of the essential preservative sodium nitrite.

George has described Denhay as 'parsimonious with salt': no more than 33g (1oz) of cure is used per 10kg (22lb) of meat. The sides of bacon are then laid in plastic boxes and left to dry-cure for two weeks. During this period they leach juices, which are drained from small holes cut into the sides of the boxes. The meat loses 30 per cent of its original weight during the cure. This contrasts sharply with some 'factory' bacon which, as George wryly observes, tends to miraculously gain weight during the curing process as it is injected with water. At the end of the cure, the salt is washed from the sides of bacon and they are suspended for two days to drip dry. They are then chilled – not frozen – cut into rashers, trimmed and packaged. It's that simple.

Flat Bake with Streaky Bacon and Vintage Cheddar

Serves 4 • A flat bake is essentially a British version of a pizza, in this case one adorned with tangy cheese and top-quality bacon. For this recipe, it would be handy to have a baking sheet the size of your oven, assuming that it is a single rather than a double one.

THE DOUGH

1 level tablespoon dried yeast (15g/³⁄₄oz)

300ml (½ pint) water, hand hot

1 teaspoon sugar

450g (1lb) strong white bread flour (we use Shipton Mill or Doves Farm)

2 level teaspoons fine or flaky sea salt (about 5g/¼oz)

2 tablespoons olive oil

THE TOPPING

2 medium red onions, thinly sliced

40g (1½oz) unsalted butter

6 sage leaves, chopped

a couple of sprigs of thyme, chopped

salt and freshly ground black pepper

200g (7oz) strong vintage cheddar, grated

150g (5½oz) Duchy Originals streaky bacon

20 cherry or baby plum tomatoes, halved

First, reactivate the yeast in half the hand-hot water (150ml/¼ pint) with a teaspoon of sugar mixed in.

Then make the dough. We recommend using a mixer. Place all the ingredients in the bowl, attach the dough hook (consult the instruction manual if necessary) and slowly knead for 2 minutes on a low setting.

Cover the bowl with a damp cloth and leave the dough to rise in a warm place (e.g. in the airing cupboard or by the Aga or a warm stove) for an hour. It should double in size.

While the dough is rising, gently fry off the onions in the butter for about 20 minutes, stirring frequently. Add the sage and thyme for the last few minutes.

Take the dough out of the bowl and transfer to your work surface. Roll it into a long sausage and divide into two. Put one half in the freezer.

Dust a little flour onto a baking sheet and roll the dough directly onto it. This will help you get the shape right – you want to cover the entire sheet – and the dough should be nice and thin.

Heat the oven to 220ºC/425ºF/gas mark 7, while allowing the rolled-out dough to rest for 15 minutes or so in a warm place covered in cling film or a damp cloth.

Spread the onions over the flat bake, sprinkle with the cheddar and artfully arrange the bacon and tomatoes.

Bake for 15 minutes until nice and crispy, and serve with a crisp salad.

Bubble and Squeak, plus Soufflé

Serves 4 • Bubble and Squeak is an evocative name for an old British dish made from potatoes, cabbage and bacon. It's traditionally made on a griddle. Though scarcely an upmarket food, it can form the basis of a surprisingly classy soufflé.

750g (1lb 10oz) organic mashing potatoes, peeled and cut into small-ish chunks and boiled until soft

250g (9oz) cabbage leaves, boiled for 5 minutes, then cooled in cold running water

180g (6oz) Duchy Originals back bacon, roughly chopped

40g (1½oz) butter or lard

salt and freshly ground black pepper

THE SOUFFLÉ
(MAKES 4 SINGLE PORTIONS)

2 tablespoons fresh white breadcrumbs (about 1 slice)

2 eggs, yolks separated

400g (14oz) bubble and squeak

40ml (1½fl oz) double cream

50g (2oz) mature cheddar, grated

flour, for dusting

a pinch of nutmeg

Drain and mash the potatoes and chop the cooked cabbage leaves into small pieces. Then fry with the bacon in the butter over moderate heat for about 20 minutes. Turn the mixture over from time to time with a slice, and add a little salt and pepper before serving.

If you want to make a soufflé, preheat the oven to 220ºC/425ºF/ gas mark 7. Blend the white bread in a food processor and whip the egg whites into soft peaks.

Grease 4 soufflé dishes with butter and sprinkle with a light layer of flour. This will help the soufflés to rise unimpeded.

Take a large bowl and combine the bubble and squeak with the double cream, egg yolks and most of the grated mature cheddar.

Fold in the egg whites and add a pinch of salt.

Combine the breadcrumbs with the last of the cheese and a sprinkling of nutmeg and work together with your fingers.

Portion into the soufflé dishes and sprinkle with the breadcrumbs.

Bake in the oven for around 10 minutes, until risen. Don't open the oven door while the soufflés are cooking, or they will collapse.

Roast Pork Loin with Sorrel Sauce

Serves 4+ • Bitter, slightly metallic and very refreshing, sorrel forms the basis of a delicious contrasting sauce which cuts through the sweetness of the pork. Sorrel grows wild in the English countryside, but is often cultivated.

THE PORK

1 rolled loin, approximately 1.2kg (2lb 12oz)

lots of salt

5 medium carrots, peeled and cut in half lengthways

salt and pepper

olive oil

1 teaspoon dried sage

THE SAUCE

80g (3¼oz) shallots (3 small to medium ones), finely diced

40g (1½oz) unsalted butter

150ml (¼ pint) white wine

75g (3oz) fresh sorrel, or 3 good handfuls, finely chopped

2 egg yolks

Score the skin of the pork with a sharp knife. Then rub plenty of salt into it and leave in a cool place for at least 2 hours.

Preheat the oven to 240ºC/475ºF/gas mark 9.

Season the carrots with salt and pepper and a little olive oil, then line the baking tray with them. If you don't have enough to fill the tray cut some more. This will prevent the ones on the outside burning

Wash all the salt off the loin and pat dry.

Mix 1 teaspoon of salt with the dry sage and 1 tablespoon olive oil and rub the mixture all over the loin.

Place the pork on a trivet above the carrots or rest it on top of them. Bake for 35 minutes until the skin has crisped up. Turn the oven down to 180ºC/350ºF/gas mark 4 and bake for a further 35 minutes.

Meanwhile make the sorrel sauce. To do this, gently fry the shallots in the butter for 5-8 minutes until soft. Add the white wine and reduce by half by turning up the heat a little.

Add the sorrel and continue to cook gently for a couple of minutes.

Remove the sauce from the heat and stir in the egg yolks and a little salt and pepper.

Leave the pork to rest for 10 minutes before serving it with the warm sauce and some sautéed potatoes and red cabbage.

Home-made Tagliatelle with Streaky Bacon and Mushrooms

Serves 4 • Tagliatelle are long ribbons of pasta. They have plenty of surface area, so they are very good at 'picking up' creamy sauces of the kind featured in this recipe. To make tagliatelle at home, follow the instructions for making pasta in the cannelloni recipe on page 43. Once you have made the dough, either process it in a pasta machine if you have one, following the instructions for tagliatelle, or roll it out into a large, thin sheet and cut it into long strips about 1cm/$\frac{1}{2}$in wide. Italians traditionally lay their tagliatelle over the back of a chair as they make them to prevent the strands becoming entangled.

If you go for the home-made option, each diner will need about 125-150g (4$\frac{1}{2}$-5oz) of tagliatelle. If you are not feeling energetic, you can always use dry pasta, in which case allow 75-100g (3-3$\frac{1}{2}$oz) per person.

As far as the mushrooms are concerned, you have a choice between regular farmed varieties (chestnut or button mushrooms) or wild species like chanterelles or ceps.

180g (6oz) Duchy Originals streaky bacon, sliced

a small pat of butter

200g (7oz) sliced mushrooms of your choice

2 garlic cloves, chopped

1 teaspoon chopped thyme

200ml (7fl oz) crème fraîche

100g (3½oz) cheddar, grated

salt and ground black pepper

Fry the bacon in the butter in a medium-sized pan over moderate heat for 5 minutes, stirring frequently.

Add the mushrooms, garlic and thyme and fry gently for another 8-10 minutes.

Add the crème fraîche and cheese. Gently simmer until the cheese has melted, season with a little pepper and salt and serve immediately with the pasta.

If you have made the tagliatelle yourself, they will need to be cooked for about 3-4 minutes (test after 3 minutes). If you are using dried pasta, follow the instructions on the packet.

Bacon and Asparagus Tart

Serves 4 with a little bit left over • Asparagus just about qualifies as a late Spring vegetable. In England, the first spears are ready in May, and they are arguably the best in the world. This is a shallow tart with a shortcrust pastry base. We recommend using a shallow 26cm (10½in) diameter non-stick pizza pan, 1cm (½in) deep with a 1cm (½in) lip.

THE PASTRY (ENOUGH FOR 1 TART)

see the cheese pastry recipe on page 204

THE FILLING

12 medium stalks of asparagus

120g (4½oz) mature cheddar

100g (3½oz) crème fraîche

2 egg yolks and 1 egg white

80g (3¼oz) Duchy Originals streaky bacon, cut into small pieces

salt and freshly ground black pepper

Blanch the asparagus in boiling water for 3 minutes. Cool in cold water and reserve.

Make the pastry, following the recipe on page 204.

Preheat the oven to 200ºC/400ºF/gas mark 6. In the meantime, roll out the pastry to the approximate size of the pizza pan. Lay the pastry over the pan and press it down. You can trim the sides if you like, but we don't bother. It just looks better that way.

Mix the grated cheddar with the crème fraîche and egg and add a little salt.

Spread the cheese mix on top of the pastry, and arrange the asparagus spears like the hands of a clock. This will make the tart easier to cut. Finally, distribute the bacon pieces and grind some pepper on top.

Bake for 15 minutes until nicely browned.

Mussels Grilled with Bacon, Spinach and Cheddar

Serves 4 • This is a great party dish. All the ingredients are thrown onto a large shallow tray and grilled until melted and bubbling. Place in the middle of the table and let everybody dig in.

You will need a large saucepan with a tight-fitting lid and a shallow tray that will fit under the grill.

300g (10½oz) spinach

1kg (2¼lb) fresh mussels

a splash of dry white wine

100g (3½oz) mature cheddar, grated

150g (5½oz) Duchy Originals streaky bacon, diced quite small

Briefly blanch the spinach in boiling water, then refresh it with cold water and squeeze out into a small green mass.

Clean the mussels, removing barnacles and beards. Look out for dead ones, which will stay ajar, and discard them.

Take a large saucepan, pour in the white wine and add the mussels. Make sure the pan has a tight-fitting lid.

Cook over unrelenting heat for about 5 minutes. All the mussels should have opened; throw away any that haven't.

Allow the mussels to cool, then take out the meat and discard the shells (you may want to save the cooking liquor for a soup or sauce).

Scatter the mussels on the grilling tray, then roughly chop the spinach and crumble on top. Sprinkle with the grated cheese and top with the bacon pieces. Then season and grill for 7-10 minutes until golden brown and bubbling.

Serve with chips and rye bread and butter.

WOODLAND

The hazel and cherry chips used to smoke the Duchy Originals delicatessen ham and free range back bacon respectively come from the Duchy of Cornwall's woodland in Herefordshire. Hazel is also used to smoke the Alaskan salmon. Sustainable forestry is an important aspect of the Duchy philosophy, so one day in early Spring we drive to the Welsh Marches to investigate.

Surprisingly, New Barn, the headquarters of the operation, is situated in open countryside. Our first question to Geraint Richards, the Head Forester, is therefore 'Where are the trees?' He laughs and assures us that we'll be seeing plenty of them shortly. Woodland accounts for about 12 per cent of the 12,000 acre estate, but the forested portions are widely distributed.

The Duchy of Cornwall purchased the estate in 2000, largely on account of the 'ancient semi-natural woodland' as Geraint describes it. He now spends his time commuting between the broadleaf forests in Herefordshire and the Prince of Wales's largely coniferous holdings in Cornwall. Geraint joined the Duchy of Cornwall in 1996, the year in which the Duchy's forestry operation became one of the first in Britain to receive FSC (Forest Stewardship Council) accreditation.

The local red clay soil is ideal for hardwoods like oak, ash, cherry, lime, hazel and sweet chestnut. Geraint's task is to ensure that all these species are able to grow together in harmony while yielding timber on a sustainable basis. The first part of the equation involves, among other things, making sure that enough light reaches the saplings and protecting them from deer and grey squirrels. Densely treed areas must be thinned out to allow the flourishing of an underlayer of hazel, which is

important both commercially and from the perspective of wildlife. The rare dormouse, for example, is hazel-dependent.

One aspect of sustainability is carefully selecting which trees to fell and when. Oaks, for example, take up to 150 years to mature, so only one in 150 can be felled in the average year. Another technique is the ancient art of coppicing. This involves cutting adult trees down to stumps and allowing several trunks to grow from them. New growth can then be regularly harvested without killing the parent tree. The procedure is effectively the arboreal version of a haircut.

We begin our tour in Aconbury Wood, which stands on high ground, commanding views from the perimeter that extend to the Black Mountains in Wales. As we walk around, we are immersed in birdsong and a deep peace descends on us. Geraint points out the various species of tree, examples of coppicing and the remnants of an Iron Age Hill Fort. He also explains how the bracken is prevented from growing too high: it is 'bruised' by a horse-drawn machine which crushes the stems without severing them. Our only regret is that the bluebells with which the forest floor is carpeted have yet to flower.

After lunch, we drive to Bucknall's Wood, a few miles from New Barn. As we approach, we hear the distinctive sound of chainsaws. This old anemone-strewn coppice wood is delightful, but was neglected by the previous owners. Geraint's two employees, Ray and Peter, are working hard to get it back in shape. We spend half an hour watching them coppice hazel before ruefully returning to the concrete jungle.

Clockwise from left Geraint Richards with Keira the dog. Hazel trunks. Woodstore with cherry wood in the foreground and hazel behind. Ray, coppicing a hazel tree. Cherry wood drying out.

Cannelloni Stuffed with Smoked Ham and Cheddar

Serves 4 • This is comfort food of the highest order and you may well find yourself eating it out of the dish with a spoon. If you have never made your own pasta, now is the time to start. However, if you are a bit short of time, you can buy perfectly good sheets of fresh pasta.

THE PASTA

250g (9oz) durum wheat flour

140g (5½oz) whole egg

THE SAUCE

500ml (18fl oz) milk

1 medium leek, sliced

1 small red onion, sliced

40g (1½oz) butter

25g (1oz) plain flour

100ml (3½fl oz) crème fraîche

50g (2oz) cheddar

a little salt and freshly ground black pepper

THE CANNELLONI

16 rectangles of fresh pasta, measuring around 10–12cm (4–5 inches) by 8cm (3in)

strips of Duchy Selections ham

strips of cheddar

THE TOPPING

any leftover cheese and ham, but no more than a good sprinkling of either

freshly grated nutmeg

You must be very precise with these quantities when making the pasta. Use flour made from durum ('hard') wheat; on the packet it will say 'semolato di grano duro'.

Place the flour in a pile on your work surface and make a well in the middle for the eggs. Whisk them in gently, gradually adding more flour until the egg has become completely incorporated.

Work the mixture into a sticky mass and continue until it becomes smooth. It is important that you use up all the flour.

Check whether the mixture is of the right consistency by sticking your thumb in. If it comes out clean, the dough is ready.

Knead the dough with the heel of your hand, half turning it, always in the same direction. Knead for at least 5 minutes.

Divide into 3 parts and follow the instructions on your pasta machine or roll out the dough thinly. Your sheets of pasta should be about 10–12cm (4–5in) by 8cm (3in).

To make the sauce, first heat the milk slowly in a pan. Do not let it boil.

Gently fry the leek and onion in the butter for 10 minutes until soft, then stir in the flour.

Slowly add the hot milk, stirring and adding the flour to thicken.

Add the crème fraîche, cheddar and a little seasoning. Simmer for 5 minutes, stirring frequently.

Reserve the cheesy leek mixture until needed. Cover with a sheet of greaseproof paper to prevent a skin from forming.

Preheat the oven to 180°C/350°F/gas mark 4.

Make the cannelloni by laying the cheese and ham parallel to the longer sides of the pasta and rolling up tightly into tubes.

Take an oven dish and pour in a little sauce. Lay a single layer of cannelloni on top, then a little more sauce, then the rest of the cannelloni. Cover with sauce and sprinkle with the extra cheese and ham and some grated nutmeg.

Bake for 20 minutes, then turn the oven up a little for 5 minutes.

Serve with chunky bread and a pile of spinach.

TURKEYS

It may be a surprise to find turkeys in the Spring chapter, but we have our reasons. Above all, we want to illustrate early in the book that farming is a year-round business, even when the end product is heavily seasonal, as in this case. We also wanted to look into the breeding operation. As the KellyBronze turkey sold by Duchy Originals is a slow-growing breed, this begins in the Spring and, to be frank, no one at Kelly's Turkeys would thank us if we pitched up anywhere near Christmas. They would just be too busy.

Kelly's farm stands in a gently undulating part of rural Essex. We arrive early one misty morning and know we have found the right place when we see the magnificent terracotta turkey cock at the end of the drive. The impression of turkeyness is reinforced in reception by photographs of the birds with all manner of celebrities, from the late Queen Mother to Larry Grayson.

Paul Kelly, the managing director, is a proud Essex man with an endearing giggle. He ushers us into a comfortable meeting room and begins to describe the business with an almost missionary zeal. Indeed, he is so enthusiastic, and things are going so well, that he sometimes comes across as a man who can't believe his luck.

The company's success is built on a remarkable bird. The KellyBronze is like the turkeys of sixty years ago, before economic forces and breeding technology combined to produce a race of giants. Whereas commercial turkeys can reach almost 40kg (88lb) in 30 weeks, the adult KellyBronze weighs about 5kg (10-11lb). It is almost

identical to the wild turkey of North America, and tastes as good as that implies. Yet there were no KellyBronzes prior to the 1960s. The breed owes its existence to the painstaking work of Paul's father Derek, who gradually reconstructed the ancestral bird after immersing himself in turkey lore in America.

The business has two separate sides: the breeding and hatching of six breeds of turkey to supply specialist farmers all over the country, and the rearing of KellyBronzes for the table. We begin our tour with the hatchery. In a few weeks, Kelly's will be dealing with 130,000 eggs per week, three-quarters of which will hatch successfully. Paul shows us into the incubator room, where the eggs are kept for 24 of the 28 days between fertilisation and hatching. Each of the giant silver machines can hold a mind-boggling 40,000 eggs and keep them at the optimum temperature.

Shortly before they are due to hatch, the eggs are transferred to hatching trays. The new-born turkeys will have absorbed so much yolk that they won't need to eat for 5 days. Although this is a quiet time at Kelly's, there is always some turnover, and we are able to observe a clutch of day-old chicks at close quarters, basking under a heat lamp. They are attractive little creatures, unexpectedly duck-like,

with a spray of feathers on their heads that will disappear within five weeks. The black ones are curiously reminiscent of penguins.

After meeting the chicks, we make our way to Paul's nearby house to have a look at some adult KellyBronzes. The majority will be eaten at Easter, which accounts for three per cent of business. The turkeys live in a large barn with direct access to a big field. They are spectacular animals, with jet black feathers and electric blue skin on their heads. The males, with their fan-tails and wattles, are particularly impressive. They look much more like exotic wild birds than their domestic status would suggest. Then, out of the blue, Paul starts gobbling. He is answered in kind by a unanimous chorus of 800 birds. We spend a happy quarter of an hour pulling the same trick.

Before we leave, Paul briefs us about the Duchy Originals turkeys. Their superlative flavour, he explains, is a consequence of their longer life-span, and the fact that the birds are dry-plucked and hung for two weeks rather than the industry-standard seven days. He also gets quite passionate about how they should be roasted. Older birds have more fat marbling than younger ones. Fat heats up more quickly than protein and they therefore require less cooking time particularly if the stuffing is cooked separately. More of that in the Winter chapter...

SUMMER

Summer is the season of peak activity for Duchy Originals suppliers, just as it is in the natural world with which their lives are so intimately entwined. In the Scottish Highlands, the Balmoral hives are transported to higher ground for the bees to feast on the heather as it comes into flower on the moors. Further south, the damsons are ripening and the fields of organic wheat and oats are beginning to change colour. The pesticide-free hedgerows that adjoin them are abuzz and aflutter with insects and butterflies. Meanwhile everyone is gearing up for the harvest...

The early part of the Summer is a bonanza for grazing animals, with the grass at its greenest and most nutritious. We begin our journey with the Home Farm cattle. There are two herds at the farm, milk-yielding Ayrshires and beef-producing Aberdeen Angus. We take a close look at both.

The next port of call is the heavily wooded Cotswold valley where the Duchy Originals soft drinks and cordials are made. Few places can be as inviting on a hot Summer day as the Bottlegreen headquarters, particularly when a tray of cool, refreshing samples is presented on arrival.

In August, we return to Home Farm to focus on the culmination of the agricultural year: the harvest. This encompasses not only the major grains (wheat, oats and barley), but also 'lesser' crops like mustard and clover, which make valuable contributions to the diets of humans and farm animals respectively. We track the progress of all the crops, starting with mustard. These lead us to one of the company's most important partners: Tracklements in Wiltshire, where the mustards and chutneys are made.

In the late Summer, we follow the oats – and Prince Charles and the other Royals – to the Highlands of Scotland. Here we visit Walkers of Speyside, manufacturers of the Duchy Originals biscuits and the world's finest shortbread. Then we journey to the wild fringes of the Balmoral estate, where we meet the bees responsible for the exquisite Duchy heather honey.

DAIRY

We arrive at Home Farm at 5.30 one pristine August morning with instructions to meet Fred, the relief milker. Instead of the wizened, Hardy-esque figure of our imaginations, Fred turns out to be a tall, young Dutchman. He introduces his dog Takkie, who is a quarter collie and three-quarters retriever. Fred says he might be of some use later on if the collie genes happen to kick in on the day.

We make our way to a steep field directly across the drive from the main farm buildings, where 135 Ayrshire cows are waiting for us nonchalantly, together with one small black Aberdeen Angus bull and a handful of recently born calves. The bull is there to 'mop up' any cows who have failed to get pregnant via artificial insemination. Ayrshire bulls are considered too big and fierce for the job; you wouldn't want to get into a field with one. The scene is absurdly idyllic, with the rising sun bathing the mottled hides of the cows in a soft, orange glow. Fred's eyes seize on an attractive yellow plant, which he promptly uproots and tosses into a hedgerow. 'Ragwort', he explains with a scowl, 'It's poisonous to cattle.'

The first task of the day is to collect a three-day-old calf (an Ayrshire/Red Angus cross) and deliver it to its mother in the 'nursing unit' next to the dairy. The small brown calf is initially chaperoned by two aunty cows. They make nervous, protective little moos as we progress, but eventually drop away with a bit of encouragement from Takkie.

When we get to edge of the field, Fred unwinds a length of tape from the spool attached to top of each gatepost, stretches it across the driveway, and hooks it to a 'mirror' gatepost on the dairy side. Once he has repeated the process with another

They are faintly reminiscent of a tube
carriage of city gents at rush hour.

pair of gates closer to the dairy, there is a seamless walkway from field to milking unit. At first we are unconvinced by the tape 'ropes', which look unlikely to contain determined half-ton cattle – they could just duck under them for a start – but this turns out to be a non-issue. As soon as the gates are opened, it becomes apparent that the cows positively want to be milked. They almost trot down the hill and make their way to the holding pen of the milking unit in a highly orderly fashion. Rather endearingly, the bull comes too. They clearly know the routine by heart.

The holding pen is pretty crowded by the time the stragglers have squeezed themselves in, but the cows bear their sometimes slightly undignified proximity with calm forbearance. They are faintly reminiscent of a tube carriage of city gents at rush hour. Then Fred pushes a button, and a pair of computer controlled barriers opens at the 'business end' of the pen. Precisely six animals are allowed to pass

through before the barriers close. Each placidly makes her way to the nearest available bay, where Fred gently attaches a suction tube to each of her teats. Three minutes later, the job is done and she is uncoupled from the milking machine. Then she walks up a ramp and disappears from view along a steel 'catwalk', like a bovine supermodel.

When the first group have all been milked, the barriers open again, six more cows shuffle into position and the cycle begins anew. It takes Fred about an hour and three-quarters to milk the entire herd, which he does solo, with music pumping out from the local radio station. While he gets on with the manual work, a computer analyses the yield from each animal, which it identifies via a microchip embedded in the blue, padlock-shaped pendant worn by all. The system allows the health of the cattle to be monitored in great detail, as well as the quantity and quality of their milk.

The average Home Farm Ayrshire produces around 5,000 litres (8,500 pints) of milk per lactation, and can expect to have seven lactations before she retires. The standard dairy Holstein, by contrast, yields 10,000–12,000 litres (17,000–20,000 pints) per lactation but is burned out after three yields. There is also a difference in the end product. Ayrshire milk is somewhat sweeter than normal, due to its high lactose content. The fat globules within it are also more uniform in size, which is thought to make it easier to digest.

Left to right Escorting cows to the dairy. Fred, the relief herdsman.
Opposite, main photograph Rush hour: Ayrshires in the dairy, waiting to go into the milking parlour. **Bottom, left and centre** The milking.
Right The cows feed on silage after their milking.

When the milking is over, we find out where the cows went after they disappeared down the catwalk, along with the little bull, who neatly sidestepped the milking machine when his number came up. They have assembled in a long, straw-filled shed, and lined themselves up along a fence of metal railings on one side. What happens next reveals the neatness of the dairy's design. A tractor drives down the centre of the shed, depositing large steaming piles of silage along the 'human' side of the fence. Then the cows poke their heads through the railings and tuck in. Having just been milked, they are ravenously hungry and eager to stack up with nutrients to furnish the next day's supply of milk. There is slightly too little fence space for all the cattle to eat at once, so there is a lot of jostling, and a few of the less dominant animals have to wait for a space to become available. The bull is very much at the back of the queue. As the animals gorge themselves,

occasionally tossing sprays of silage into the air, we seek out numbers 24 and 50, of which Fred is particularly fond.

After the herd has finished breakfast, we repair to David Wilson's kitchen for our own. Not surprisingly, milk figures prominently at the table. Unlike the Duchy Originals product sold in the shops, it is not pasteurised, so David dutifully 'reads us our rights', even though he knows it is more than healthy. It is, of course, extremely good. David

aptly describes it as 'liquid life'. He explains that this impression is greatly enhanced if it is drunk at body temperature, straight from the cow. The milk destined for the public is pasteurised in Somerset in line with health and safety regulations, but it is not homogenised. As a result the cream rises to the top naturally, in the traditional manner. Homogenisation is the process in which most of the milk sold in the UK is forced through small holes to rupture the fat cells.

THE BASE

16 Duchy Originals oaten biscuits

40g (1½oz) soft brown sugar

75g (3oz) butter, plus some extra for greasing the tin

THE FILLING

4 eggs, yolks separated from the whites

150g (5½oz) caster sugar

200g (7oz) crème fraîche

400g (14oz) full-fat cream cheese

vanilla essence

the zest of 1 lemon

Baked Cheesecake

Serves 6 • Everyone loves a good cheesecake and baked ones have a meltingly soft texture, far better than those where the ingredients are simply piled on top of the biscuit base. For this recipe you will need a spring-release tin about 24-26cm (10-11in) in diameter.

Preheat the oven to 180°C/350°F/gas mark 4.

Place some butter on the end of your finger and wipe it around the inside of the tin. This will help the cheesecake to rise.

Blend the oaten biscuits, brown sugar and butter in a food processor until as smooth as possible.

Pour the mixture into the cake tin and tamp down using the solid base of a ramekin (or similar implement).

Whip up the egg yolks and the sugar with a whisk. Add the crème fraîche and whisk until smooth. Then whip in the cream cheese until the mixture is smooth once again.

Add a couple of drops of vanilla essence and the lemon zest.

Whip up the egg whites into soft peaks and carefully fold into the mixture. This adds air, which gives the cheesecake its lightness. Then pour the mixture into the tin, over the biscuit base.

Bake for 20 minutes, then turn the heat down to 150°C/300°F/ gas mark 2 for another 40 minutes.

This cheesecake is divine served with fresh English strawberries.

Home-made Yoghurt with Wild Strawberries

Makes ½ litre (18fl oz) of yoghurt • Yoghurt-making at home used to be a common activity. An airing cupboard was almost considered empty without a bowl of fermenting full-cream milk.

Milk doesn't last very long when the sun shines on it, and in the Middle East goat's and sheep's milk have been naturally fermented for thousands of years, originally in animal skins. The locals soon discovered that 'jugurt' was delicious and had better keeping qualities than milk. What they didn't know was the reason. Yoghurt is more acidic than milk, with a pH of around 4.5 rather than 6.5. This deters undesirable microbes, but positively encourages the growth of 'good' bacteria, chiefly lactobacillus. The result is extremely healthy: residents of yoghurt producing areas are renowned for their longevity.

When making yoghurt, the most important thing is to keep your equipment sterile to prevent unwanted bacteria getting in. Another important factor is the twelve-hour wait. Why bother, you may ask, when you can buy perfectly good natural yoghurt from the supermarket? We have three answers. Home-made yoghurt works out at less than half the price, is much creamier and tastier, and is very satisfying to make.

EQUIPMENT

a stainless-steel, plastic or glass measuring jug

1 cooking thermometer, measuring down to around 40°C (100°F)

a saucepan

a warm place (ideally 30–40°C/85–105°F), for instance the cupboard next to the Aga or the airing cupboard, OR a wide-necked vacuum flask

INGREDIENTS

500ml (18fl oz) Duchy Originals or other whole milk

1 tablespoon live yoghurt (unflavoured)

top-quality strawberries, preferably wild. Bilberries (wild blueberries) make a luscious alternative.

Sterilise your measuring jug, thermometer and vacuum flask (if using) by immersing them in boiling water for 10 minutes, then measure out the milk and pour it into a saucepan.

Slowly heat the milk to 90°C (190°F), stirring occasionally. Then cover the pan and allow the contents to cool to 50°C (120°F).

Place a tablespoon of plain yoghurt in the measuring jug and stir in the milk in two stages, a little at first, then the rest of it.

Cover the jug and leave it in a warm place for 6 hours. If you don't have somewhere suitable, pour the cultured milk into a wide-necked vacuum flask, screw the lid on tightly and leave for the same period. After 6 hours, transfer the warm yoghurt to the fridge, either sitting in the measuring jug or poured into a bowl and covered if you have used a vacuum flask.

Leave the yoghurt in the fridge for another 6 hours, during which time it will thicken further.

Stir in the strawberries or bilberries before serving. Yoghurt also goes very well with our home-made muesli (see page 69).

Ice Cream with Duchy Originals Lemon Curd

Makes 1.75 litres (3 pints) • There are two ways to go about combining ice cream with the Duchy's velvety lemon curd. The simple method is to defrost some vanilla ice cream partially and swirl in a generous portion of lemon curd. The slightly more complicated method is to make your ice cream from scratch with the lemon curd incorporated. You don't need an ice-cream machine for this recipe, which will set and freeze in the freezer, but you do need a sugar thermometer and a small pan.

3 yolks from large organic eggs

75g (3oz) caster sugar

150ml (¼ pint) water

½ teaspoon vanilla essence

550ml (19fl oz) double cream

300g (11oz) Duchy Originals lemon curd

Whip the egg yolks in a large bowl until pale and bubbly. Reserve.
Place the sugar and water in a small pan and bring to the boil. When the solution starts to thicken, insert your sugar thermometer. You are looking to remove the pan from the heat when the temperature reaches 110ºC (225ºF). It will stay at 100ºC (210ºF) for quite a time, but will then start to creep up quite rapidly and you need to be alert or the mixture will overheat.
Remove the pan from the heat and slowly pour the contents into the reserved egg yolk, whipping constantly. You should end up with a thick, slightly runny, pale yellow mousse.
Add the vanilla essence to the cream and whip until it flows, but only just.
Fold the cream into the egg-yolk mixture, swirl in the lemon curd using the blunt end of a chopstick and freeze in an airtight container.
Remove the ice cream from the freezer 10 minutes before you plan to eat it.

Asparagus Soup

Serves 4 • In England we grow the best asparagus in the world, or at least that's what we like to tell ourselves. This delicate early Summer soup could be made with asparagus 'sprue', the thinner stalks and the twisty ones that don't fit in the bunch.

100g (3½oz) onion, diced (or about half a medium one)

2 sticks of celery, about 100g (3½oz), sliced

a small leek, washed and sliced (approx 80g/3¼oz)

30g (1¼oz) butter

1.1 litres (2 pints) chicken stock or water. If you use water, mix in 2 teaspoons (10g/½oz) vegetable bouillon

400g (14oz) peeled, diced potatoes. Don't use new ones – you want a mashing potato as its function is to thicken the soup

400g (14oz) asparagus, trimmed and thinly sliced. Reserve the tips in a separate container

120g (4½oz) cheddar cheese, grated

salt and freshly ground pepper

a handful of chopped chives

Gently fry the onion, celery and leek for 15 minutes in the butter, using a saucepan with the lid on and stirring occasionally.
Add the water or chicken stock (remembering the bouillon if you are using water), then the potatoes. Bring to the boil and simmer for 20 minutes until the potatoes are soft. Halfway through the boiling add the asparagus, but not the tips.
When the potatoes are done, blend the soup until smooth, then pour in the asparagus tips and simmer for a couple of minutes.
Stir the cheese into the soup until it has melted, then season with salt and pepper.
Serve immediately garnished with chives and warm Duchy Originals bread on the side.

BEEF
CATTLE

Home Farm maintains a small herd of Aberdeen Angus beef cattle and the animals are reared organically. These are exclusive beasts, their meat destined for the likes of The Ritz and Fortnum & Mason in London.

We park up in a lush field and are immediately surrounded by a crowd of inquisitive adolescent Aberdeens. David impulsively suggests that we spend some quality time in their company. Somewhat tentatively, as the young cattle are small but muscular, we climb out of the Land Rover and select a relatively pat-free patch of grass. Then we settle down and wait. Gradually and equally tentatively, the cows begin to approach. They stop a few feet away, from which distance we can smell their pleasantly sweet breath. Then the two species spend several minutes just staring at each other. The animals' gentle curiosity is reassuring, and as we all relax, their individual personalities start to emerge. They don't remotely all look the same, and there is a lively intelligence in those big black eyes. The encounter is rather hypnotic, and it leaves us elated.

As we drive away, we realise that the Angus cattle are not the only breed represented in the field. David points out two British Whites and a tiny Shetland, its short legs reflecting generations of adaptation to life on a small island. Among its many other functions, Home Farm is a repository of rare or neglected breeds. Animals like these are living gene banks. The British Whites and Shetlands are also kept for meat, because as David says, 'you need to eat them to keep them alive.'

Beef Sauté

Serves 4 • This sauté can be made from virtually any cut of beef. Fillet, sirloin or rib-eye steak produce particularly good results.

This dish doesn't take long to cook, looks impressive and provides a hearty rustic feast. You will need to equip yourself with a large wok.

750g (1lb 10oz) new potatoes

4 medium carrots, peeled and sliced length ways

12 baby shallots, peeled

olive oil

3 large flat capped mushrooms (e.g. Portabellos), thickly sliced

at least 10 sprigs of thyme

salt

500g (18oz) of beef or steak, cut into strips

freshly ground black pepper

a glass of red wine

1 tablespoon balsamic vinegar

2 tablespoons mushroom ketchup (buy in a deli or supermarket)

a fistful of flat leaf parsley, roughly chopped

Cut the potatoes into hefty chunks and boil for 15 minutes until cooked. Drain.

Fry the carrots and shallots in a little olive oil over fairly fierce heat until nicely browned (approximately 8 minutes). Add the mushrooms and fry on for a further 5 minutes until cooked. Reserve the mixture in a dish near the stove. Repeat the performance with the drained potatoes, frying them hard for about 10 minutes in a tablespoon of olive oil along with the thyme and a large pinch of salt. Reserve.

Season the steak with ground black pepper and fry in a little olive oil until nicely browned (around 5 minutes).

Pour in the red wine, add the balsamic vinegar and mushroom ketchup, and heat over a medium flame until the liquid has reduced in volume by half.

Throw the reserved vegetables back in the wok or frying pan and toss them around for a minute or two to bring them up to heat.

Serve immediately, garnished with the parsley.

Seared Beef Salad

Serves 2 • This dish has a vaguely Oriental feel — one can imagine being served something similar in Thailand — but the ingredients are thoroughly British.

3 medium beetroot

200g (7oz) sirloin or fillet steak

1 tablespoon horseradish sauce, preferably home-made (see opposite)

2 spring onions, sliced

4 medium carrots, peeled and roughly grated

a splash of balsamic vinegar

salt, pepper and olive oil

First boil the beetroot for 30 minutes, then drain. Once it has cooled enough to handle, peel (the skin should come off easily enough) and roughly grate.

Season the beef with a little salt, pepper and a dab of olive oil.

Then fry it in a griddle pan over quite a fierce heat for a matter of minutes (3 or 4 maximum if you like it rare, 8-10 minutes for medium). Alternatively, use a chargrill or barbecue. Reserve.

Combine the horseradish with the grated beetroot, mix in the spring onions, carrot and balsamic vinegar.

Slice the beef and serve immediately with the beetroot salad.

This salad is delicious warm, but can also be enjoyed cold.

Sirloin Sandwich with Grilled Onions and Sage

Makes 2 sandwiches • This sandwich is simple but luxurious. We find it works best with thick slices of toasted Duchy Originals malted oat bread, but feel free to substitute your favourite loaf.

1 medium onion, sliced into rings

25g (1oz) unsalted butter

a dash of balsamic vinegar

4 sage leaves, chopped

1 sirloin steak, about 300g (10½oz), seasoned with a little salt and pepper and cut into 2 equal pieces.

4 slices of Duchy Originals malted oat or your own choice of bread

2 thick slices of Duchy Originals stilton

a few baby spinach leaves

Gently fry the onions in the butter with a splash of balsamic vinegar, stirring occasionally. After 10 minutes add the chopped sage leaves and remove from the heat.

Fry the beef over quite fierce heat, or use a griddle pan or barbecue. Give it 3-4 minutes if you like it rare, 8-10 for medium, and 10-12 for well done.

While the beef is cooking, toast and butter the bread. Lay a thin layer of spinach leaves on one slice per sandwich.

A minute before the steak is ready, place a slice of stilton on top so that it melts slightly.

Place the steak on the layer of spinach and cover with the onions. Cap with the top slice and cut each sandwich diagonally into four sections with a sharp knife.

If the mood takes you, wash down with a bottle or two of Duchy Ale.

Horseradish Sauce

Makes 2 jam jars • This tongue-tingling sauce features in a couple of our recipes. The horseradish used by Tracklements (see page 76) grows wild on the banks of the River Humber, but cultivated roots are available from good greengrocers.

150g (5½oz) horseradish, peeled and finely grated

200ml (7fl oz) chicken stock

200ml (7fl oz) double cream

1 teaspoon salt

40g (1½oz) fresh white breadcrumbs (about 3 slices of fresh white bread, crusts cut off, blended into soft crumb)

2 x 300ml (½ pint) jars with airtight lids

First sterilise the jars and lids by immersing them in boiling water for 10 minutes.

Heat the horseradish, chicken stock and double cream in pan and simmer for 5 minutes, stirring frequently.

Add the salt and the breadcrumbs.

Whisk for 5 minutes over low heat until the breadcrumbs have thickened the sauce.

Pour into the two sterilised jars and seal immediately. As soon as the horseradish has cooled, move the pots to the fridge.

The sauce will keep for up to 2 weeks, but as soon as the seal has been broken you must eat it within 5 days.

CEREAL HARVEST

To get a full picture of the harvest at Home Farm requires two trips: a 'before' and 'after'. We make the former in late July, when the fields are swathed with mature grain. When we return in three weeks, many of them are cleanly shorn.

On the day of our 'before' visit, we arrive to find the staff engaged in an aspect of the harvest that is easily overlooked, but central to the Home Farm system. They are making silage. The exact identity of this substance has always been a mystery to us, beyond it being reflexively blamed for the 'farm smells' that sometimes penetrate the cars of urbanites driving in the country. Yet there is nothing unpleasant about this stuff. It consists of fermented red clover. The plant has already done the farm a service by returning nitrogen to the soil and providing grazing for the animals. Now it is about to be transformed into high quality Winter fodder.

Silage, as David Wilson neatly explains, is sauerkraut for cows. The clover is cut when its sugar content is at a maximum and driven to an area next to the main farm buildings. This is what is happening around us: two tractor-loads of sweet, freshly mown clover arrive while we are present. The plants are transferred to huge open silos, where they are compacted and covered with black plastic, which is then weighed down with old tyres. The resulting pressure generates an ideal environment for anaerobic respiration. Beneath the surface, benign microbes begin to feed on the sugars in the clover and it starts to ferment. The mature silage is much more nutritious than hay, and even tastes relatively good to humans, as we find to our astonishment when David offers us a handful (see photograph on page 18).

We move on to have a look at the crops that will be furnishing human menus. The 'big three' at Home Farm are wheat, oats and barley. Rye is also grown, but it has less

Left to right The baling process. Mature heads of wheat. The baling tractor progressing down the field.
A combine harvester in action. Finished bales of hay await collection.

relevance to the Duchy Originals story. The wheat, which when milled will be used to make biscuits, is a forty-year-old variety called Maris Widgeon. It is fast-growing and long-stalked, features that allow the young plants to outstrip any weeds as they grow. This renders the use of herbicides unnecessary. Wheat is the hungriest of the crops grown at Home Farm, so it is planted directly after the three-year clover phase of the rotation cycle (see page 18), when the soil is at its most fertile. The seed is sown in Autumn, and the adult wheat is harvested in late July or August.

Oats are the next grain to be grown in the cycle. After the wheat in a particular field has been harvested and the straw baled, a 'catch crop' of turnips, forage brassicas and mustard is planted. These plants provide good ground cover between September and the following Spring, helping the soil to retain the nitrogen not used up by the wheat. They also provide Winter grazing for sheep. Then, in March, the field is ploughed and Spring oats are sown. They are harvested in August, and then make their way to Scotland where they are used in the Duchy Originals biscuits (see pages 98-101).

In the sixth year of the cycle, the field is used to grow beans. These provide high protein fodder for the cattle, and also return some nitrogen to the soil. Then, in the Spring of the seventh year, the final crop is planted. This is either Winter rye or Spring malting barley. Both plants thrive in relatively low nitrogen soil, and are well suited to the end of the rotation cycle. The rye will be sold to a local mill and thence to specialist bakers; it also provides excellent bedding straw for the livestock. But we concentrate on the barley, because it is a key ingredient in the Duchy Originals ales (see pages 133-134). The variety grown on Home Farm is called Plumage Archer, and until recently it was all but extinct. Plumage Archer is low yielding, but produces a superior malt. Its presence on the farm is a clear vote for quality over quantity.

As we make our bumpy way around Home Farm, the visual differences between wheat, oats and barley finally become clear to us. Ears of wheat are hairless and tightly packed, whereas oat grains grow separately, like diamonds suspended from a sparse arrangement of yellow wires. Barley heads are like greener versions of wheat, but they are hairy and make fun, aerodynamic darts. The name Plumage Archer seems particularly apt, as we discover during an impromptu pitched battle.

We pause in a bean field and marvel at the insect life to which it plays host. The teeming array of beetles would be a red rag to most conventional farmers, but at Home Farm they are taken as a sign of healthy biodiversity. One of the cornerstones of the organic approach is a confidence that Nature will take care of many agricultural 'problems' if left to her own devices. In a system where everything is allowed to eat everything else, with a bit of strategic management, crop pests attract birds and other predators and the problem largely take cares of itself. Meanwhile, the countryside thrives and the consumer can eat food uncontaminated by chemical herbicides and pesticides.

A few weeks later, David is, by his own admission, a distracted man as we sit down to a breakfast of boiled eggs. The harvest is like a military campaign, a mixture of careful planning and rapid response to the whims of the weather, which frequently pull in opposite directions. Nevertheless, David finds time to drive us out to the front line.

The Land Rover emerges into a humpbacked field of wheat already half-shaved by a busy combine harvester. There are a lot of buzzards in this part of the country, and one of them rises from the fringing hedgerow with lazy flaps of its enormous wings, mewing to its unseen partner. As the combine scythes through the wheat, the air fills with an earthy, stubbly scent.

Prior to the 1980s, the stubble would have been burned in a spectacular late Summer ritual, but concerns about air pollution and the possible spread of fire have put paid to the traditional practice. Contrary to what one might think, field-dwelling animals tended to cope rather well with stubble burning. When the flames died down, all kinds of creatures – hares, hedgehogs, mice, adders – would emerge from their holes and scamper or slither across the smouldering fields.

Now stubble is simply ploughed back into the soil. David Wilson understands the reasoning behind the change in the law, but cannot hide a smidgeon of nostalgia. He also has to work harder to compensate for the loss of the carbon-rich stubble ash.

When the combine has finished its work, a tractor takes over, pursued by gulls even though we are many miles from the sea. As it criss-crosses the field, the tractor leaves a trail of large, round bales in its wake. The straw will play an important role in the Winter diet of the farm animals and provide them with comfortable bedding.

Elsewhere on the farm, the oat harvest is in full swing. Once they are harvested, both the wheat and oat grains are transported to nearby Shipton Mill to be ground. A majority of the resulting flour then makes its way to the Walkers factory in Scotland, where it will be baked into the famous oaten biscuits with which Duchy Originals made its debut.

Opposite Ripe Drummer oats. **Above left** Grains of Maris Widgeon wheat.
Right A field of Plumage Archer barley. **Bottom** Golden wheat.

Scones for Full High Tea

Makes 8 • This version of high tea - there are many others - consists of scones with strawberry conserve and clotted cream, plus crustless cucumber and smoked salmon sandwiches made with Duchy Originals bread. This quintessentially British fare is ideal on a warm Summer's afternoon whether or not the vicar calls round.

You can probably take care of most of the components yourself, but here we show you how to make the scones.

an 8cm (3in) round cutter

50g (2oz) butter

250g (9oz) plain flour

½ teaspoon salt

1 teaspoon bicarbonate of soda

2 teaspoons cream of tartar

1 tablespoon caster sugar

a pinch or two of ground cinnamon

150ml (¼ pint) milk

50ml (2fl oz) crème fraîche

50g (2oz) plump raisins (optional)

Preheat the oven almost as far as it will go (230-240ºC/450-475ºF/ gas mark 8-9).

Rub the butter, flour, salt, bicarbonate of soda, cream of tartar, caster sugar and cinnamon together in a large bowl.

Add the milk, crème fraîche and raisins, if using, and stir until you have a sticky dough.

Turn it out onto a lightly floured surface and knead briefly. Then flatten the dough with the heel of your hand until it is about 2.5cm (1in) thick. Take your round cutter, dust it with flour to prevent the dough sticking to it, and cut out your scones. Brush the tops of the scones with any remaining milk.

Place the scones on a non-stick or silicone baking sheet and bake for 10 minutes. Then turn the oven off, and leave the scones inside for a further 5 minutes without opening the door (you may want to peek through the oven window a couple of times during this period to check that the scones aren't burning).

Remove the scones from the oven and leave them to cool on a wire rack.

To complete the spread, serve with some elegant sandwiches, a pot of tea and some Duchy Originals shortbread.

English Muffins

Makes 12 muffins • Until the arrival in the UK of the tall risen cakes known in America as muffins, what is now called an English muffin was simply known as a muffin. Muffins are one of the easiest risen breads to make. They are also terrific to eat, and children love them.

an 8cm (3in) round cutter

500g (18oz) unbleached white bread flour

2 teaspoons salt

15g (¾oz) fresh yeast (which freezes well, so don't worry if you have too much)

400ml (14fl oz) lukewarm milk

25g (1oz) melted butter

semolina or rice flour for dusting

Mix together the flour and salt in a large bowl. Take the fresh yeast and rub it in with your fingers. Pour in the milk and the melted butter.

Give the mixture a good stir. It will become firm and elastic after a minute or two.

Scrape the sides of the bowl down with a plastic scraper so that the dough becomes a domed mass.

Lay a damp tea towel on top and leave to rise in a warm place for 45 minutes to 1 hour until the dough has approximately doubled in size.

Scrape the dough out in one piece onto a lightly floured surface and throw a little flour on top of it.

Next, you need to deflate some of the large bubbles that have been formed by the yeast. This is called 'knocking back'. You do it by pressing down firmly on the dough with the heel of your hand. You want the whole thing to end up about 1.5-2cm thick (½-¾in).

Cut out as many muffins as possible with the cutter. Then sprinkle a flat tray with semolina and carefully place the muffins on it. Throw a good covering of semolina on top of them. Cover with a damp cloth and leave to rise for 20-30 minutes.

Place the pan or griddle on low to moderate heat and dry fry the muffins for 5-7 minutes until nicely toasted on each side.

If you decide to freeze the uncooked muffin dough, don't forget to cut them through the middle beforehand so that you don't have to defrost them before toasting.

Home-made Muesli with Oats, Wheat and Barley

Makes 4–5 servings • Making muesli at home brings out the mad scientist in us. It is all about blending your favourite dried ingredients to create contrasting but harmonious flavours and textures. Best of all, once you have finished making it you can store it in a jar and enjoy it anytime. Muesli is also extremely good for you.

The recipe below represents our favourite combination, but once you've got the hang of it you'll be combining dried fruits, nuts and grains like there's no tomorrow. The raw materials are readily available from health stores and good supermarkets.

To make one jar, you will need:

50g (2oz) flaked oats

50g (2oz) flaked barley

2 tablespoons whole almonds

2 tablespoons pecans

50g (2oz) toasted wheat flakes

4 dried figs, chopped

2 tablespoons chopped dates

2 tablespoons dried cranberries

2 tablespoons flaked coconut

2 tablespoons green pumpkin seeds

2 tablespoons sunflower seeds

2 tablespoons chopped dried apple pieces

3 tablespoons raisins

Preheat the oven to 180ºC/350ºF/gas mark 4.

Pour the barley and oats onto a baking tray and bake for 15 minutes in a thin layer. Bake the almonds and pecans for 10 minutes, and allow all the hot ingredients to cool.

Using your hand, mix all the ingredients together in a large bowl, then pour immediately into a sealed jar.

Keep in a cool, dry place and use within 2 months.

Bramley Apple and Blackberry Pie

Serves 6 • In Britain, blackberries are thick on the bush in late Summer and early Autumn. They are free, ubiquitous and particularly good when cooked. Unfortunately, too many go to waste because people don't realise how well they freeze. We avoid this problem by loading up our freezers with blackberries during the picking season.

This recipe should be made in a greased pie dish. The one Nick uses is 21cm (8in) across and 5cm (2in) deep.

THE PASTRY

200g (7oz) plain flour

75g (3oz) butter

50g (2oz) icing sugar

1½ large eggs (to divide an egg in half lightly whip and divide into 2)

a couple of drops of vanilla essence

THE FILLING

300g (10½oz) blackberries

400g (14oz) diced Bramley apples, cooked slightly to soften

120g (4¼oz) soft brown sugar

1 heaped tablespoon Duchy Originals damson preserve (or appealing substitute)

1 egg, lightly whipped

Make the pastry in a large bowl. Rub the flour, butter and icing sugar together for about 5 minutes with the tips of your fingers, then stir in the eggs and vanilla essence with a spoon.

Turn the pastry out onto your work surface, knead lightly, and mould it into a sausage.

Divide the 'sausage' into 2 unequal blocks, one a third of its weight and one two-thirds. Store the pastry in the fridge until needed.

Preheat the oven to 200ºC/400ºF/gas mark 6. Meanwhile, roll out the larger piece of pastry and line the pie dish with it, letting any excess overlap over the sides.

Mix the filling ingredients together in a bowl. Spoon the mixture into the pie dish and brush the pastry rim with the whipped egg. Then roll out the lid (the smaller piece of dough) and place it on top of the pie. Press the edges of the rim and lid together and trim off any excess pastry. Then egg-wash the lid with a brush, and prick the pie in several places to prevent it exploding during cooking.

Bake for 20 minutes, then lower the heat to 180ºC/350ºF/gas mark 4 for a further 20 minutes.

Serve with vanilla ice cream or clotted cream.

BREAD

The majority of Duchy Originals suppliers are based in the countryside. La Fornaia is different. The surroundings are far from bucolic: the headquarters are just off London's North Circular Road, a stone's throw from Wembley Stadium, and the bakery is as big as an aircraft hangar. Nevertheless the company ethos is entirely in harmony with the Duchy philosophy. Despite the size of the place, the atmosphere is friendly and 'human' and the dedication to quality is palpable. The ovens and dough mixers may be industrial in scale, but every product is hand-finished.

La Fornaia means 'lady baker' in Italian. The previous owner was indeed female and a baker, though not particularly Italian. The name also reflects the company's cosmopolitan workforce (there are nineteen nationalities represented on the staff). True to form, we are greeted by a lady baker; this time from New Zealand. Her name is Shirani and she works with the Duchy Originals team. She's also friendly, efficient and well-informed. When we ask the first question on our list, namely what distinguishes the Duchy breads from other organic breads, she answers with impressive certainty. 'They are healthy but indulgent', she says with a smile. It occurs to us that this wouldn't be a bad motto for Duchy Originals as a whole.

La Fornaia bakes five kinds of bread for Duchy Originals: wholemeal, sunflower seed and honey, malted oat, mixed seed and vintage cheddar. The current best-seller is the mixed seed loaf, closely followed by the sunflower seed and honey bread, but

From top to bottom Sunflower seed and honey bread. Mixed seed loaf. Vintage cheddar cheese bread. Malted oat loaf. Wholemeal bread.

today is a cheese bread day, so this is the variety on which we focus during our tour. Johnny, who hasn't had breakfast, is delighted. He knows from previous experience that the Duchy vintage cheddar bread is more than good enough to eat on its own.

When we first enter the bakery, it smells of slightly sweet dough, although Shirani tells us that the aroma varies. We walk through the storage and mixing rooms, and into the cutting room where the prepared dough is divided into loaves. The cheddar bread is the only one in the Duchy Originals range that isn't baked in specially designed oval 400g (14oz) tins. Instead, it is shaped by hand. All La Fornaia products are hand-finished, but the Vintage Cheddar Bread demands an extra level of dexterity. Not only are the loaves manually rolled; they are rolled two at a time. We watch in admiration as a young baker makes a pair of perfect examples in a matter of seconds, one with each hand. The dough he uses, however, is portioned out by a sophisticated machine. To combine technology with human input in this way is a feature of La Fornaia.

When the loaves have been shaped, a star shape is cut into each with three strokes of a knife, and precisely 18g (¾oz) of grated vintage cheddar is sprinkled on top. At the time of our visit, the cheese in question comes from the Alvis family, who produce West Country cheddar of the highest quality at their family farm at the foot of the Mendip Hills, a few miles from the village that gave the cheese its name. After they have received their topping, the raw loaves are transferred to an enormous steel proving oven, where they spend

'They are healthy but indulgent', she says with a smile.
It occurs to us that this wouldn't be a bad motto for
Duchy Originals as a whole.

15-20 minutes at 35°C (95°F). This temperature encourages maximum yeast activity, which causes the dough to rise. The other Duchy Originals breads are proved when the dough has risen to the lips of their tins, but there is no such reference point in the case of the vintage cheddar bread, so the timing is a matter of judgement.

Once they are proved, the loaves are baked for 24 minutes at 240°C (460°F) in huge rotary ovens. They are then wheeled to the coolers, although at this stage Shirani and JP, the production manager, have mercy on Johnny and hand him a warm cheese loaf. When the other loaves have cooled, they progress to the packaging area.

Having seen the cheddar bread safely packaged, we move on to the preparation area, which is located in a sectioned-off corner of the warehouse. This is where the doughs for the other breads in the Duchy range are mixed, divided and rolled. All these operations are carried out by an ingenious machine. As the bread is formed, the loaves rise upwards along a spiral pathway like passengers on a reverse helter-skelter. When they reach the top, they are placed on a table and hand-topped. We linger in the preparation area, opening the lids of numerous storage bins and inspecting their contents. These range from sunflower, pumpkin and poppy seeds to fragrant honey and olive oil. Most of the seeds, we are told, are sourced from organic suppliers from around the world, the climate in Britain not being suitable for growing the parent plants.

When we get back to the meeting room, we find that Shirani has arranged for us to meet the Chief Executive and the Sales Director.

The former, rather wonderfully, is called Peter Baker, the latter Ken Glennon. They have come to tell us about the business side of the business, as it were. La Fornaia's relationship with Duchy Originals began almost as soon as they bought the company in 1996. By March of that year, they were baking Duchy Originals bread for the supermarkets. The original brief, Peter explains, was to make good bread that happened to be organic rather than the converse. The use of organic ingredients was, of course, of paramount importance to Duchy Originals, but the company had no desire to sell breads that were worthy but dull. La Fornaia has stayed true to that maxim, and today Duchy Originals accounts for a seventh of the firm's considerable business.

Over the years, various changes have been made to the Duchy Originals range, including the increase of the standard size of the loaves from 300g to 400g (11oz to 14oz). Before we leave, Ken outlines the searching development process to which potential additions to the Duchy line are subjected. Of a current shortlist of about 15 candidates, he expects two or three at the most to make it to market.

Johnny lives fairly near the bakery, but the still warm vintage cheese loaf has entirely disappeared by the time he gets home. Nevertheless, he manages to retain loaves of each of the other Duchy Originals breads (wholemeal, sunflower seed and honey, malted oat and mixed seed), and later hands them over to Nick to experiment with. Nick makes a glorious Bread and Butter Pudding, which appears on page 94.

Opposite Various stages of bread production, from the rolling and scoring of the dough for the vintage cheddar bread (top left), to the oats for the malted oat bread and the seeds for the mixed seed loaf just before baking (centre and main photograph, right) and the finished loaves and packaging (bottom).

MUSTARD

Yellow mustard is one of the most rewarding crops grown on Home Farm, both visually and in terms of contribution to the cook's flavour bank. It also plays a valuable role in maintaining the fertility of the fields in which it is grown. Mustard plants draw up nutrients, which are ploughed back into the soil along with the stalks after the harvest, and thus made available for future crops. The seed is harvested in August. It is then cleaned by a local firm called Churches, using an ingenious Victorian contraption, and driven to The Tracklements Company in the neighbouring county of Wiltshire.

When we meet Guy Tullberg, the managing director and son of the founder, our first question is how the company came by its name. Tracklements turns out to have been the term used by his paternal great-grandmother, who hailed from Lincolnshire, for chutneys, pickles and other goodies typically served with meat. ('Could you pass the tracklements please?') When Guy's father, William, started the business, he remembered his grandmother's expression and adopted it for his company.

William Tullberg was a butcher who started making his own wholegrain mustard in 1970. He had to eat a lot of pies and sausages in his line of work, and had grown weary of the two varieties of mustard then available in the UK to accompany them: yellow (English) and brown (French). So he dug up a recipe in John Evelyn's seventeenth-century *Diaries*, and made up a batch in a plastic dustbin. He gave a jar to a friend, who in turn passed it on to a local landlord, and soon he was swamped

Tracklements turns out to have been the term used by
Guy's paternal great-grandmother for the chutneys,
pickles and other goodies typically served with meat.

with requests for more. William rented a room in the market town of Calne, near his Wiltshire home, and began to make mustard commercially. He subsequently left his job and opened a restaurant, which provided him with an opportunity to experiment with other condiments. Before long, the infant company had diversified into chutneys, relishes and dressings, and outgrown the original premises. The current site near Sherston is the third.

Guy is an exuberant and extremely tall man – like a surprisingly high proportion of his staff, he is six foot four plus – and he clearly adores making 'tracklements'. After a few minutes on the shop floor, we begin to understand why. The air itself is appetising, filled with spicy and fruity aromas, and the mixing process is pleasingly hands on. In various parts of the room, vegetables are being chopped and oils blended into dressings, but we keep our eyes on a steaming kettle of Duchy Originals tomato chutney. This delicious concoction, made with organic tomatoes, onions, dates, Bramley apples, spices and cider vinegar, is slow boiled for ninety minutes in small batches. All that remains is for the chutney to be bottled, which happens in another corner of the unit.

We now turn our attention to the wholegrain mustard. This is made from cider vinegar, honey, spices and two kinds of mustard seed. The white seed, which hails from Home Farm, provides the nasal sensation when the mustard is eaten. The plants only grow to half the height of the inorganically farmed equivalents, but as David Wilson tells Guy, 'that's nitrogen for you'. The brown seed, which comes from America, is responsible for the heat on the tongue. It is sourced from the USA for a simple reason: once established, brown mustard plants are

impossible to get rid of, so British farmers, who are relatively strapped for space, are reluctant to grow them.

Both seeds are stored whole, as are the spices, because this allows them to retain their essential oils for up to year. Were they powdered, they would lose their potency within weeks. The ingredients are ground at the last minute, and mixed with cider vinegar before any flavour is lost. The mixture is then stirred with a wooden paddle in a 'Hawaii Five-O' motion. At first, it is very liquid, but it rapidly thickens as the ground seed swells. We take turns putting our faces in a half-finished barrel of Duchy Originals mustard, and are hit by a pungent, acrid wind. As anyone who has ever overloaded a forkful of food with mustard knows, too much of it can be overwhelming, but it is delectable in small quantities.

The striking thing about Tracklements is how 'human' the manufacturing process is. It is people rather than machines, for example, who decide when the products are ready, and they judge by feel and experience rather than readings from dials. The high acidity of the products pre-empts the need for artificial preservatives, and the batch sizes are small enough to allow plenty of experimentation. Tracklements can easily produce bespoke or one-off lines, which gives the firm great flexibility.

Before we leave, Guy shows us the library. The family – Guy's wife Kate is the development chef – has accumulated a splendid collection of old recipe books and they are a perennial source of inspiration for new 'tracklements'. Guy draws our attention to the volume of *John Evelyn's Diaries* that first moved William Tullberg to make mustard, and, gratifyingly, to a copy of our previous book *Preserved*.

Opposite, top row Mustard seed is poured into the grinding machine. **Centre** Supervision of the grinding process.
Bottom left Bottling the mustard. **Bottom right** Proud MD Guy Tullberg.

Home Farm Salad

Serves 4 • The point of this salad is to showcase classic garden veg. It can be served cold or warm. We prefer it warm because the flavours meld better than way. If the salad has been refrigerated, leave it out for half an hour before you eat it.

12-15 baby carrots, cleaned

a small bunch of asparagus, trimmed

10-12 runner or stringless beans, trimmed

6 rashers of Duchy Originals streaky bacon, chopped

olive oil

4 large flat mushrooms, sliced

a teaspoon of chopped, fresh thyme

½ a red onion, sliced

a small handful of roughly chopped flat leaf parsley

salt and freshly ground pepper

Duchy Originals honey and mustard vinaigrette

Boil up a large pan of water. Blanch the carrots, asparagus and beans for 5 minutes, then lightly refresh them in cold water.

Fry the bacon in a little olive oil over moderate heat for about a minute, then add the mushrooms with the salt, pepper and thyme and cook through.

Toss all the ingredients in a large bowl, remembering the red onion and parsley, and serve with Duchy Originals honey and mustard vinaigrette.

Sausages Baked with Organic Wholegrain Mustard and Honey

Serves 3 • These sausages are baked with a sticky sweet and savoury coating on a non-stick baking tray. They are delicious on their own, but try them in a sandwich or with mashed potatoes and onion gravy.

6 Duchy Selections pork and herb sausages

2 heaped teaspoons dried marjoram

1 teaspoon mustard powder

30g (1oz) Duchy Selections honey

30g (1oz) Duchy Originals wholegrain mustard

20g (¾oz) tomato ketchup

a generous twist of black pepper and a pinch of salt

Preheat the oven to 150°C/300°F/gas mark 2.

Mix all the ingredients together apart from the sausages. Place the sausages on a non-stick baking tray and spoon the gooey mixture evenly on top.

Bake in the oven for 25 minutes, raising the temperature to 180°C/350°F/gas mark 4 for the last 5 minutes.

If there is any goo left at the bottom of the tray, mop it up with bread because it's too good to waste.

English Herb Salad

Serves 4 • This aromatic chopped herb salad is perfect for picnics. Other adjectives which come to mind to describe it are fragrant, heady, healthy and refreshing.

a couple of handfuls of rocket leaves, roughly chopped

20 purple basil leaves

a handful of flat leaf parsley, roughly chopped

2 handfuls of mustard leaves, chopped

a handful of chervil

a small bunch of chives, roughly sliced

a few tarragon leaves

10 cherry tomatoes, sliced in half

Duchy Originals honey and mustard vinaigrette

Mix all the salad ingredients together in a large bowl and serve with the vinaigrette.

SOFT DRINKS

In Prince Charles's youth, he was particularly close to his great-uncle Lord Louis Mountbatten, who introduced him to a drink traditionally given to thirsty harvest workers on his family's estate in Kent. It was a zesty, old-fashioned and extremely refreshing lemonade. The Prince was very taken with it, and the Lemon Refresher has since been adopted as a family drink. It is also one of a family of soft drinks and cordials made for Duchy Originals by Bottlegreen near Stroud in Gloucestershire.

The Bottlegreen factory is situated where it is for two reasons: elderflower, which forms the basis of many of the drinks, is locally abundant and the site has its own supply of pure water. Specifically, there is a bore-hole under the car park. It was drilled on the advice of an 82-year-old dowser, who detected water fifty feet underground after the company had spent a fortune on fruitless geological reports.

The firm's speciality is applying wine-making skills to the production of soft drinks. Kit Morris, the founder, and his wife Shireen established Bottlegreen in 1989 with the aim of developing a top-quality English elderflower wine. Chris Baker, the chief blender/product development officer also has a wine-making background. The firm was flexible enough to change tack when it became apparent that soft drinks promised a better commercial future, but the legacy is obvious in the staff's liberal use of terms like 'palate', 'balance' and 'body'.

Simon Speers, the managing director, explains that the emphasis at Bottlegreen is firmly on purity. He is immensely proud of the company's filtering system, which, for the technologically minded, is effective to the level of 0.2 microns (a micron is a millionth of a metre). After several glasses of the results, we are entirely convinced. Particularly impressive is the latest Duchy Originals product, a strawberry and mint cordial that captures the essence of Summer.

Once we are thoroughly refreshed, Simon leads us into the blending room. This, as the name implies, is where the ingredients for all the cordials, pressés and carbonated drinks are mixed prior to bottling, and, in the latter case, carbonating. Earlier in the day, the staff prepared three batches: one of Lemon Refresher for Duchy Originals and one each of red and white grape juice. The ghosts of their aromas fill the blending room, along with those of the various essences, concentrates and distillations that have preceded them. The combined scent is strongly reminiscent of boiled sweets.

We move into the bottling plant, where we watch the company's enormous pasteuriser in action. Weirdly, the machine is absorbing green Duchy Originals bottles at one end but spitting out red ones at the other (they contain grape juice). The paradox is resolved when we learn that it takes each bottle 63 minutes to pass through the pasteuriser, during which time it is heated to kill off any mould and yeast spores in its contents. Clearly a batch of red grape juice has been succeeded by one of Lemon Refresher during the past hour.

Our tour ends in the laboratory, where samples from every batch of drinks are kept in quarantine for three days. This allows them to be closely monitored for yeast growth and other undesirable developments. The lab is also where new drinks are dreamed up. Jackie, one of the product development officers, shows us around. Then we amaze our nostrils by waving samples of a bewildering array of concoctions and essences beneath them.

Bottlegreen currently makes seven kinds of soft drink for Duchy Originals: four carbonated refreshers (lemon, apple, ginger and elderflower) and three cordials (elderflower, ginger, and strawberry and mint). They are refined adult drinks, delicious on their own but also excellent as mixers and in cocktails. We leave with armfuls of each, eager to explore the possibilities.

Above Hundreds of green bottles, not hanging on a wall.

Left Labels for the lemon refresher.

Whisky Refresher

This variation on the whisky sour is an easy cocktail to make but also one of the most addictive.

Serve your whisky refresher in a straight-sided tumbler of around 250ml (9fl oz), which is called an Old Fashioned in the trade.

50ml (2fl oz) whisky (any kind you like, but purists would be shocked if you used malt)

lots of ice

a bottle of Duchy Originals lemon refresher

a lemon, cut into slices

Pour the whisky into a tumbler and add plenty of ice and a good squeeze of lemon.

Top up with lemon refresher and garnish with a lemon wedge. We defy you not to have a second.

Duchy Iced Tea

Forget Long Island Iced Tea and try the Duchy Originals version. As with its American cousin, the name of this cocktail is somewhere between euphemistic and downright misleading: Duchy Iced Tea contains no tea and is extremely alcoholic.

This recipe yields 4-6 decent drinks. Mix it in a 1.2 litre (2 pint) jug which you have previously chilled in the freezer and serve it in highball glasses.

40ml (1½fl oz) gin

40ml (1½fl oz) vodka

40ml (1½fl oz) tequila

40ml (1½fl oz) Grand Marnier

40ml (1½fl oz) dark rum

lots of ice

a bottle of Duchy Originals lemon refresher

a few slices of lemon

Take the jug out of the freezer and pour in the alcohol. Add plenty of ice and top up with lemon refresher and a few slices of lemon.

Balmoral Fling

This close relative of the Singapore Sling is another cocktail best mixed in a pre-frozen 1.2 litre (2 pint) jug and then served in highball glasses.

150ml (6fl oz) gin

25ml (1fl oz) grenadine

loads of ice

a bottle of Duchy Originals apple refresher

75ml (3fl oz) Calvados

some maraschino cherries

a few slices of green apple

Remove the jug from the freezer and pour in the gin, grenadine and ice. Top up with apple refresher and gently float in the Calvados by pouring it in just above the meniscus (the surface of the liquid). **Serve** in highball glasses, garnished with the apple slices and cherries.

Highgrove Strawberry Daiquiri

This is a virgin cocktail, that is to say one which contains no alcohol. You could add rum and strawberry liqueur to make a real daiquiri, but this is a wonderfully refreshing Summer drink as it is.

You will need a relatively heavy-duty blender to crush your ice, otherwise you'll have to wrap it in a clean tea towel and bash it with a mallet or rolling pin. As per usual, you should make up this cocktail in a pre-frozen 1.2 litre (2 pint) jug.

12 medium strawberries (make sure they're in season rather than imported or forced)

juice of 1 lime

a bottle of Duchy Originals lemon refresher

10 large ice cubes, crushed

more strawberries for garnish

Blend the strawberries with the lime juice, 100ml (3½oz) of the lemon refresher and the crushed ice until smooth. If you find you haven't got quite enough liquid to make it blend smoothly, add a little more refresher.

Pour the delectable red slush into the jug and gently stir in lemon refresher until it is full.

Garnish with slices of strawberry and serve in highball glasses.

Home Farm Cooler

This light cocktail is like a Cosmopolitan, but with Apple Refresher instead of lime juice. Once again you should make it in a pre-frozen 1.2 litre (2 pint) jug.

200ml (7oz) vodka

plenty of ice

cranberry juice

a bottle of Duchy Originals apple refresher

a lime

some watermelon slices

Take the jug out of the freezer and pour in the vodka. Add lots of ice and top up with cranberry juice and apple refresher. Serve in straight-sided tumblers with a squeeze of lime and a garnish of watermelon.

500ml (18oz) Duchy Originals
lemon refresher

2 tablespoons caster sugar

3 heaped teaspoons powdered
gelatine

1 lemon, skinned and cut with
a sharp knife into tiny pithless
segments

a punnet of raspberries

double cream

Lemon Jelly with Raspberry Cream

Serves 4–6 • This tangy jelly is shockingly tasty, slightly fizzy and makes a wonderful Summer dessert. You could also serve
it as a highly modish between-course palate cleanser, in which case make smaller portions and leave out the raspberries and
cream.

Line 4 to 6 ramekins with cling film.

Heat 150ml (¼ pint) lemon refresher in a saucepan with 1 tablespoon
of sugar. When the mixture comes to the boil, remove the pan from
the heat. Sprinkle in the gelatine and whisk hard until it has dissolved.

Add the rest of the lemon refresher and the small lemon pieces. The
liquid will fizz up. Stir it a few times, then pour into the ramekins,
and put them in the fridge until set.

To make the raspberry cream, place the raspberries in a pan along
with the second tablespoon of caster sugar. Bring to the boil, then
pass through a sieve to get rid of the pips.

Allow the raspberry coulis to cool, then swirl it around on the set
jellies and top with some cream.

BEES & HONEY

Duchy honey is made from nectar harvested from wild heather in the Scottish Highlands. Most of it is produced between July and mid-September, so one day towards the end of the season we fly to Aberdeen, jump in a car, and head off to meet the beekeeper. When Murray McGregor arrives for our rendezvous in the small town of Ballater, a short drive from the Balmoral Estate, he confronts us with an interesting dilemma. His van broke down earlier this morning, and in his haste to borrow a vehicle, he forgot to bring any spare safety equipment. All of us are a little nervous, and for Jonathan the photographer, who needs to take close-ups, this is potentially very bad news.

Ever resourceful, we decide to improvise. First, we pick up masking tape and some marigold gloves in a hardware store. Then we buy some midge netting in one of the 'huntin', fishin' and shootin'' shops in which the area abounds. Jonathan may end up looking like an extra from a zero-budget movie, but at least he will stand a chance.

Murray is an instantly likeable man, big, deadpan and well-informed. As we drive away from Ballater, he explains that he looks after about 1,600 hives, each with around 35,000 inhabitants. This translates to one bee for every head of the UK's population. He also informs us, to our considerable surprise, that London, where we have just come from, is the most productive region for honey in the UK as there are lots of flowers and not many bees. He won't have it that it is any less good than the rural equivalent, because he knows how effectively bees filter out pollutants.

We turn off the main road into one of the many tracks with which the area is criss crossed and which Murray knows like the back of his hand. The route takes us through rare patches of primary Caledonian forest. As the track climbs, we pass salmon fishers on the River Dee, and head up one of its tributaries, the Muick. We stop off to look at a pair of salmon ladders, constructed on either side of a waterfall to facilitate the progress of the fish to their spawning grounds, and catch a glimpse of Birkhall, the former Summer residence of the late Queen Mother, through the trees.

After a few miles, we park up and are led into a sheltered grove of Scots pines. The first insects to make their presence known are the midges, which are rather too numerous. Then we spot a group of about thirty hives. They are as simple as they could possibly be, consisting of stacks of unpainted wooden frames. Each frame arrived supporting a 'foundation sheet' of hexagonally impressed wax to provide the bees with a template for cell building. The more storeys a hive has, the older it is. Murray tells us that colonies can keep going indefinitely, but in practice he loses about 15 per cent of his bee population per annum.

Realising that we are in the right kind of environment, Johnny asks Murray if there are any capercaillies around, and if so, whether he has any advice on cooking them. Capercaillies are giant cousins of the grouse, notorious for tasting of pine needles. The beekeeper takes him aside and says 'an old gamekeeper taught me an excellent recipe

for capercaillie', which he pronounces to rhyme with 'paper daily'. 'You take your bird, go into a forest and dig a hole. Then you put the bird in the hole, and cover it with earth and pine needles'. It takes quite a while for the penny to drop that Murray has finished his story.

The second group of hives are clustered in open country, with a backdrop of heather-clad hills. They look ancient and solemn, like a row of Tibetan altars. The exposed position of the hives prompts us to ask Murray about bees and weather. He informs us that they only emerge when the temperature reaches about 10°C (50°F), but keep the interior of their hives at a constant 37°C (98°F) by huddling together. This enables honey bees to survive temperatures of forty below on the Canadian prairies, but as Murray wryly explains, they have to keep their legs crossed for months on end as they won't excrete in their hives.

As we walk back to the cars, Murray points out the two kinds of heather that provide the raw materials for the worker bees. Bell heather is purple, with relatively large flowers that appear earlier in the Summer. Ling heather is pink and later flowering. The honey made from their combined nectars is very three dimensional in taste, the Bell supplying the richer notes and the Ling the sharper ones.

Our journey to the third city of bees takes us through some seriously wild country. Murray draws our attention to stone cairns atop some of the peaks, many of them erected by Queen Victoria and Prince Albert. He also entertains us with translations of the earthy

Gaelic names of the most prominent mountains. Then, in the apparent middle of nowhere, we find ourselves in a village that could have been teleported from 1930s rural Hampshire. We have reached Balmoral. Unfortunately, there has been a confusion about dates, so the constable stationed near the post office respectfully directs us to turn back. Murray grunts and almost immediately finds a back route that allows us to circumvent the village.

We are soon back in wooded country. By now we have no idea where we are, but we are here to see more bees. This is where we get stung. The trip begins promisingly enough, with a short walk to a collection of hives surrounded by ferns. All of us bar Murray and Jonathan keep about twenty yards away, because one of the hives is to be opened up for photographs, but we feel perfectly secure. Murray even plays a trick on Johnny, handing him what turns out to be a live bee, but thankfully a stingless drone. At that moment, the taller of your authors discovers the appropriateness of the expression 'bee line'. With impressive single-mindedness, a member of the colony launches herself from the hive, heads straight for Johnny's neck and deposits her sting before he has any idea what is happening. To everyone's amusement, he tears off his upper clothing and runs away. Murray removes the sting with the lightest flick of a thumbnail, and Johnny basks in his initiation.

It is rather less funny when a few bees gets inside Jonathan's improvised face-net. Fortunately, he is only stung twice, but when Petra, the Duchy Originals press officer, receives similar treatment, we decide this might be a good time to leave. As Murray says, perhaps a little gratuitously, 'they're getting a wee bit stroppy now'.

The final group of hives on our agenda is situated in a broad, steep-sided valley, next to a meadow of heather and beneath some noble Scots pines. As we approach, Murray points out a patch of rare white heather. Despite the loveliness of the setting, Nick, Johnny and Petra elect to stay in the car. Jonathan has no such luxury, but on this occasion he has the consolation that Murray will be using his smoker. This home-made device will make the bees sleepy, but not harm them or their honey in any way.

The wind is getting up, but as we watch the beekeeper and photographer at work, we hear distant stags barking between gusts. When Murray and Jonathan return to their cars, they bring us a freshly extracted comb of honey. Murray cuts open the wax cells and a glowing jelly oozes out, which we immediately spread on some oatcakes. They are very more-ish and we eat rather a lot. Then we say goodbye to Murray with sticky handshakes and head back to Aberdeen.

Relatively little happens to the honey itself between hive and shop shelf. As Murray says 'It's the bees that make the honey, not the beekeepers'. The freshly harvested product is essentially ready to eat and beyond improvement. It is so pure that heat-treatment, which would damage the texture, is entirely unnecessary. The honey is separated from the comb by a centrifuge, bottled, and that's about it.

Bread and Butter Pudding

Serves 4+ • This classy version of the classic British pudding will bring tears of joy to the eyes of ex-boarding school pupils. It will also delight everyone else.

Bread and butter pudding is actually best made with slightly stale bread. You should eat it as soon as it is cooked to take full advantage of the caramelised top.

You will need a pie or rectangular dish with a capacity of about 1.5 litres, (2½ pints) and a cooking thermometer.

8 slices of Duchy Originals sunflower and honey bread, crusts sliced off, if you like

unsalted butter

150g (5½oz) fresh wild bilberries or blueberries

300ml (½ pint) milk

100ml (3½fl oz) crème fraîche

½ teaspoon vanilla essence

1 level tablespoon Duchy Selections honey

2 large eggs and 1 egg yolk

50g (2oz) brown sugar

1 teaspoon ground cinnamon

Preheat the oven to 120°C/250°F/gas mark ½.

Spread each slice of bread with butter, then cut into triangles.

Place a layer of bread at the bottom of the dish, followed by a handful of blueberries. Repeat until you have used up all the bread and fruit. Make sure there are some blueberries on top, as they will merge deliciously with the brown sugar under the grill.

Heat the milk, crème fraîche, vanilla essence and honey in a saucepan to around 70°C/160°F (use a cooking thermometer).

Whip up the eggs and half the sugar in a large bowl until frothy. Whisk in the milk and pour the mixture over the bread and blueberries. Leave to rest for 10 minutes to allow the liquid to soak into the bread.

Sprinkle the rest of the brown sugar over the pudding and powder with ground cinnamon. Bake for 45 minutes. Then pop it under a preheated grill for 4-5 minutes to brown and caramelise it.

Serve with clotted cream or just au naturel.

Balmoral Honey Cake

Makes a cake yielding 10–12 good slices • This delightful cake is soft, delicate and light and incredibly easy to make. It is perfect for afternoon tea and will keep well in an airtight tin for a few days.

You will need a large bowl and a medium-sized cake tin with a removable base.

a little butter for greasing

flour for dusting

100g (3½oz) light muscovado sugar

200ml (7fl oz) crème fraîche

200g (7oz) ground almonds

100g (3½oz) Duchy Selections honey

1 large egg, white separated from yolk

175g (6oz) flour

2 teaspoons baking powder

Preheat the oven to 165ºC/330ºF/gas mark 3.

Grease the cake tin with butter and dust with a thin layer of flour to make a non-stick barrier.

Whisk the muscovado sugar together with the crème fraîche in a large bowl. Stir in the ground almonds, honey and egg yolk. Then sift in the flour and baking powder and give the mixture a good stir. Finally, whip up the egg white into soft peaks and gently fold into the cake mix.

Spoon the mix into the cake tin and bake for 40–45 minutes. Ovens tend to vary, so check that it is not cooking too fast after 20 minutes or so.

If you are not sure whether the cake is ready or not, insert a wooden cocktail stick into the centre. If it comes out covered in cake mix, you need to cook it for a little longer.

Transfer the cake onto a wire rack to cool, and store in an airtight container.

Flapjacks with Balmoral Honey

Makes enough for around 12 portions • This recipe produces a moist flapjack, full of oats and seeds. You will need a small baking tin (25 x 18cm/10 x 7in is ideal) and some baking parchment.

100g (3½oz) rolled oats, roughly blended in the food processor

25g (1oz) green pumpkin seeds

25g (1oz) sunflower seeds

75g (3oz) soft brown sugar

150g (5½oz) unsalted butter

75g (3oz) Duchy Selections honey

Preheat the oven to 150°C/300°F/gas mark 2.

Mix the oats, pumpkin seeds and sunflower seeds and soft brown sugar in a large bowl.

Melt the butter and honey together and pour over the rest of the ingredients. Mix thoroughly with a large spoon.

Line the baking tin with the parchment and spoon in the flapjack mix. Pat down, then bake for 25-30 minutes.

Take the flapjack mass out of the oven and allow it to cool. Peel off the baking parchment and slice into portions.

Your flapjacks will keep in an airtight container for up to a week.

BISCUITS & SHORTBREAD

Our second destination in Scotland reveals what happens to a good portion of the oats and wheat harvested at Home Farm. Flour from both grains is lucky enough to wind up in the village of Aberlour, by the River Spey, where it is converted into the Duchy Originals biscuit and shortbread range. Walker's Shortbread is one of the finest biscuit manufacturers in the UK and has been making the definitive Highland shortbread for over a century.

The drive from Aberdeen to Aberlour takes us past fields of the biggest-looking cattle we have ever seen, and then up into whisky country, where many of Scotland's venerable distilleries are clustered. Speyside is a long way from Gloucestershire, but the partnership has been mutually rewarding, both commercially and in terms of quality, since the very beginnings of the Duchy Originals story. It was here that the oaten biscuit with which the brand made its debut was developed in the early 1990s. Today, Walkers makes 15 different kinds of organic biscuit for Duchy Originals.

Most of the range is represented on the enticing tray which Phyllis, who meets us at reception, later brings into the boardroom. We are there to meet Jim Walker, joint managing director and grandson of the founder. Our first question concerns something that has long puzzled us: what exactly is short about shortbread? Jim explains that the term originally meant 'easily broken', which bread baked with sugar certainly is compared with the regular stuff. He goes on to reveal that the shortbread on which Walkers built its success has just four ingredients: flour, butter, sugar and a little sea salt.

Our first question concerns something that has long puzzled us: what exactly is short about shortbread? Jim explains that the term originally meant 'easily broken'.

The butter is the key. Walkers gets all its supplies from the British Isles, and specifically from producers whose cows spend the greatest percentage of the year grazing on grass. The company only uses fresh butter and always tries to incorporate as much of it into its biscuits as possible, hence their creamy taste. Jim ruefully points out that not all manufacturers are so scrupulous. To qualify legally as shortbread, it merely has to have a fat content of at least 24 per cent, and many other manufacturers use margarine. Jim pronounces the word with a hard 'g', enhancing the impression that he isn't a fan of the practice.

The complete Duchy Originals range consists of three kinds of oaten biscuit - traditional, with cracked black pepper, and with rosemary and thyme - two shortbreads (Highland and butterscotch), and several wheat-based but non-shortbread biscuits. They include 'plain' varieties flavoured with lemon, orange and ginger respectively, plus two covered with milk chocolate – coconut and butterscotch – and two with dark chocolate – ginger and orange. Finally, there are the cheese nibbles. These savoury morsels come in three flavours: cheddar, rosemary and thyme, and mustard. Walkers goes to great lengths to acquire the best organic ingredients. The ginger, for example, is bought from Buderim in Queensland, which is held by the cognoscenti to produce the finest in the world. Similarly, the lemons are sourced from Sicily and the orange peel from southern Italy because these are the places where the most aromatic fruits are grown.

The factory to which we proceed smells delicious. Particularly interesting are the 'dies'. These are giant rollers, made of gleaming bronze, which impress the patterns on the biscuits. Each one costs as much as a new car. Naturally, the die used for the Duchy Originals range grabs our attention. It is responsible for the logo, based on the Duchy of Cornwall's heraldic crest, which is imprinted on all the brand's biscuits apart from the chocolate ones.

At the end of our tour, Jim shows us some of the memorabilia the company has collected over the years. Walkers is not just a company; it is a repository of Highland culture. Pride of place goes to the painting of Bonnie Prince Charlie and Flora MacDonald that has long adorned the company's biscuit tins. In 1998, Jim got a call from Sotheby's to say that the original picture was coming up for auction. The board deemed it well worth spending the £70,000 necessary to secure it. Jim is almost as proud of a photograph of him as a child standing next to an enormous fish. The salmon, which had just been caught by his father, remains the largest ever landed on this section of the River Spey.

On departure, we are weighed down with biscuit samples and presented with an excellent book on the Highlands published by the company. As we walk back to the car, two red squirrels hop onto the verge. Before we leave Aberlour, we stop off at the original Walkers shop on the other side of the village which was opened by Jim's father in 1910. It is overflowing with uniformed teenagers from the local school, just as it will have been for almost a century of lunch hours. Walkers evidently continues to play an integral role in the life of the community.

Opposite, left Various stages of the biscuit-making process. Note the lovely, crumbly texture (second row) and the gleaming dies which stamp the Duchy Originals crest on the biscuits (bottom row). **Right** Orderly rows of biscuits emerge from the oven.

Ginger Nuts

Makes 35–40 biscuits • This recipe produces a soft, chewy ginger nut. These biscuits must not be overcooked or they will lose their 'juiciness'. Duchy Originals don't currently sell ginger nuts, but if they did, they would be as good as these.

You will need a silicone sheet or a well-greased baking tray and a wire rack.

150g (5½oz) light muscovado sugar

50g (2oz) sesame seeds

15g (¾oz) dried ginger

50g (2oz) desiccated coconut

150g (5½oz) golden syrup

150g (5½oz) unsalted butter

200g (7oz) plain flour

Preheat the oven to 140ºC/290ºF/gas mark 2.
Combine the sugar, sesame seeds, ginger and desiccated coconut in a large bowl.
Melt the golden syrup and butter together, and combine with the above ingredients.
Add the flour and stir into a thick paste.
Pick up a little bit of the dough with a tablespoon and roll into a ball (a 15-20g (½-⅓oz) ball will make a medium-sized biscuit).
Place the balls of biscuit mix on the baking tray, quite well spaced because they will spread during cooking.
Bake immediately for 15 minutes. You don't want the biscuits to brown. If they do, you are cooking them for too long or on too high a heat.
When the biscuits come out of the oven they are a little flimsy so let them rest for a minute or two before you transfer them to cool on a wire rack.
The ginger nuts will keep very well for a week or two in an airtight container.

Apple Crumble with Highland Shortbread

Serves 4–6 • This crumble puts others to shame, thanks to the buttery shortbread and the Calvados. Using shortbread produces a classier crumble than the traditional method of rubbing butter, flour and sugar together. It is equally delicious with vanilla ice cream or custard.

THE CRUMBLE

300g (10½oz) Duchy Originals shortbread biscuits, crushed in a food processor or with a pestle and mortar

40g (1½oz) unsalted butter, softened

THE FILLING

5 medium Bramley apples, peeled and roughly diced

100g (3½oz) seedless raisins

½ teaspoon ground cinnamon

60g (2½oz) Duchy Selections honey

90g (3½oz) light muscovado or soft brown sugar

a shot or two of Calvados

Preheat the oven to 150ºC/300ºF/gas mark 2.
Crunch and crumble the crushed biscuits into the butter until you can't see the butter anymore.
Mix the apples with the raisins, cinnamon, honey, sugar and Calvados in a large bowl.
Spoon the mixture into a pie dish and sprinkle evenly with the crumble.
Bake for 1 hour. For the last 5 minutes, turn the oven up to 200ºC/400ºF/gas mark 6. The pudding should emerge golden brown.
Serve with ice cream or custard.

AUTUMN

The cereal harvest is over by the time Summer gives way to Autumn and much of the British countryside lies freshly ploughed. Other crops, however, are only now reaching maturity. The orchards that supply the raw materials for the Duchy Originals preserves are heaving with fruit and the spotlight in the fields shifts below ground to root vegetables. September is also the month in which the organic First Gold and Target hops that flavour the Duchy Originals ales are harvested in Worcestershire and Kent.

We begin this chapter at Crabtree & Evelyn in Somerset, where the preserve makers are busily harnessing the fruits associated with this time of year. We then return to Home Farm to observe the root vegetable harvest. Next, we spend a wonderful day at the Wychwood Brewery in Oxfordshire. Finally, we go fishing in Cornwall. The local mackerel fishery is active at all times of year except the Spring, when the fish spawn, but donning sou'westers and heading out to a cold sea feels quintessentially autumnal.

A couple of the recipes in this chapter are game-based, namely game pie and potted venison. We have included these recipes for three reasons. First, game is highly compatible with the company ethos. Although pheasants and deer, like other wild foods, cannot be classified as organic, they lead healthy, natural, outdoor lives. Second, eating game is thoroughly in tune with the season, and its management makes an important contribution to the maintenance of the countryside. Finally, the recipes are extremely good, if we say so ourselves.

PRESERVES & MARMALADE

Crabtree & Evelyn's preserve factory is set in a beautiful part of Somerset, just past the Quantock Hills as approached from Bristol and the East. Driving there is a pleasure in itself. We are greeted by the general manager Bob Cummins and his equally affable colleague Toni Reed, who is in charge of business development, and led into a meeting room to hear the Duchy Originals story.

Although the firm is well known for its cosmetics, which it has been manufacturing for more than thirty years, Crabtree & Evelyn is also an established name in the world of preserves. As Bob explains, the quality production of both relies on similar biochemical expertise. The company has been making up and bottling Duchy Originals' preserves, honeys and marmalades since 1997, and is currently doing so at a rate of more than a million jars per annum. Before its partnership with Duchy, Crabtree had no experience of organic production. Today, organic preserves account for the majority of the factory's business.

Toni and Bob are quick to point out that much of their work for Duchy is dependent on the caprices of Nature. There will, for example, be twice as much honey from the Balmoral estates in a good year than one in which the heather flowers are damaged by unseasonable frost in Scotland in July or August. Similarly, the British damson harvest can vary wildly: in 2003, it failed almost completely as the result of a sustained spell of humid, mould-encouraging weather. Had the damsons been doused in pesticide and fungicide, the effects would have been ameliorated, but this is of course a non-option in the case of organic fruit. The risky nature of the organic approach makes Duchy preserves seem even more precious.

Our visit coincides with the manufacture of a product less vulnerable than most to yearly swings in supply: marmalade. Crabtree makes three varieties of marmalade for Duchy Originals: Clementine, Sicilian blood orange and Seville. Today is a Seville day. We begin our tour in the storage area, where the oranges arrive from Spain in bin-sized containers. The fruit has been pasteurised and pre-cut according to Duchy Originals' specifications. Because the oranges are so acidic, the sealed containers have a shelf-life of eighteen months, and can be stored at ambient temperatures. Soft fruits, on the other hand, tend to arrive and be stored frozen to maintain their integrity.

After washing and clothing ourselves to comply with the company's stringent hygiene requirements, we make our way into the heart of the factory: the food production unit. This is effectively a hermetically sealed box within the larger box of the storage warehouse. A sign near the entrance proclaims 'organic production only'. Inside, the air is almost literally thick with the bitter-sweet aroma of cooking oranges.

Bob and Toni take us through the various stages the oranges must undergo before they emerge as jarred marmalade at the other end of the unit. First, they are emptied into a tray and visually checked for blemishes. Then they are combined with organic sugar and transferred to huge, copper-bottomed boiling pans. As Diane (pictured opposite) and her colleagues stir the hot mixture with paddles, tiny marmalade stalactites form on the rims of the pans.

After boiling, the acidity of the marmalade is checked and a refractometer is used to assess how well the fruit has absorbed the sugar. Then it is transferred into a holding tank with a capacity of eight 60-80kg (130-170lb) batches, and piped to the bottling area at 90°C (190°F) This is done by means of a special pump designed not to damage fruit tissue. Finally, the marmalade arrives at the filling machine, where it is squirted into sterilised jars. These then pass through a metal detector and on to the capping and labelling areas.

Having seen the marmalade-making process in its entirety, we turn our attention to the other items in the Duchy Originals range, namely six preserves (strawberry, raspberry and lime, English damson, Morello cherry, Summer fruit and blackcurrant) and a velvety lemon curd. The latter, which has won several awards, is made with organic eggs, unsalted butter and Sicilian lemon juice. The dairy component of the lemon curd gives it a shorter shelf-life than the other Duchy preserves – nine months as opposed to two years – but you would need an iron will to refrain from consuming a jar long before that time has elapsed. Toni is particularly fond of eating the curd when it is still warm and has yet to set.

The preserves are all made in roughly the same simple manner. Before the batches are cooked up, the staff carry out preparatory setting tests to make sure the end products will have the right consistency. Each batch contains 25kg (55lb) of sugar, a similar quantity of fruit (the exact proportion depends on variables like juiciness), a little citric acid and pectin, which is a natural setting agent, and a teaspoon of sunflower oil. The function of the oil is to prevent the pans from boiling over, but it all burns off during the cooking process. The company also makes a point of incorporating whole fruits of varying sizes into its preserves to give them interesting and satisfying textures.

Crabtree goes to great lengths to purchase the best organic fruit. Ideally, it is sourced in Britain – indeed the Damson Preserve has helped revive demand for this venerable fruit, which was previously often left to rot on the ground for want of a suitable market – but this is not always possible because British farmers tend to grow varieties for the table rather than those that stand up best to cooking. Other ingredients come from all over the world. The best organic strawberries and blackcurrants for preserve making are Turkish and Danish respectively. The raspberries that hold their shape best when cooked are 'Wilhemettes', which are also particularly brightly coloured. There are also fruits that cannot be grown in Britain. The limes used in the raspberry and lime preserve are from Sri Lanka and the Caribbean, and the blood oranges and clementines used in the marmalades come from Sicily and Spain respectively. The Crabtree buying operation, then, is thoroughly international, yet the preserves are definitively British.

Opposite Marmalade production. Diane, production supervisor at Crabtree & Evelyn. Adding organic sugar to the fruit. Weighing out the uncooked marmalade. Stirring the heating marmalade in a boiling pan. Testing a sample for quality and pH. Marmalade stalactites forming around the rim of a boiling pan.

Profiteroles Stuffed with Whipped Lemon Curd

Serves 6 + • Regular cream-filled profiteroles are good enough as it is, but they are even better stuffed with tangy lemon curd and drenched in the zesty sauce below. You will need a mixer with a whisk attachment for this recipe and a silicone or well greased baking sheet.

THE PASTRY

250g (9oz) whole egg (about 5 eggs, but you need to be precise)

120ml (4fl oz) Duchy Originals or other good organic milk

120ml (4fl oz) water

1 teaspoon fine salt

2 teaspoons caster sugar

110g (4oz) unsalted butter

140g (5oz) flour

THE FILLING

200ml (7fl oz) double cream

200g (7oz) Duchy Originals lemon curd

THE SAUCE

80ml (3fl oz) lemon juice

finely shredded lemon zest from 1 lemon

80g (3oz) caster sugar

Preheat the oven to 220ºC/425ºF/gas mark 7.

To make the pastry, begin by weighing out and lightly whisking the eggs. Leave them by the mixer.

Pour the milk, water, salt, sugar and butter into a saucepan and bring to the boil. Reduce the heat to low and sift in the flour, stirring it in with a wooden spoon to make a paste.

Transfer the paste into the mixer bowl and turn the machine on at a slow setting. Pour in about ⅕ of the egg, turn up the mixer and when the egg is incorporated slow it down again. Add a bit more egg and repeat the process until all of it is used up. You will have a viscous but smooth paste.

Take a teaspoon of paste, then lay the blob onto the baking sheet. Repeat until the baking sheet is covered with blobs, keeping them at least 2cm (¾in) apart. Bake for 12 minutes, then turn the oven down to 180ºC/350ºF/gas mark 4 and bake for a further 15 minutes with the oven door slightly ajar to help to dry out the profiteroles. This is essential if they are to set and not collapse. If they are undercooked it will be a disaster – they will be soggy and flat.

Remove the profiteroles from the oven and leave them to cool.

You may now want to make another batch, as the mix yields about 3 shelves worth in a normal-sized oven. Don't worry if you don't use all the profiteroles up, as they freeze very well. Just make sure you defrost them and refresh them in the oven for a few minutes.

To make the filling, whip the double cream until just pourable but not stiff, then fold in the lemon curd.

Now make the sauce. Pour the lemon juice, zest and sugar into a saucepan and boil over moderate heat for 5 minutes until a syrup has formed. If you have a food thermometer, the desired maximum temperature is 108ºC (225º).

Cut into each profiterole with a sharp knife and then insert some whipped curd using a teaspoon or piping bag. Pour the warm syrup over them and consume immediately.

Trifle with Organic Morello Cherry Preserve

Serves 6 • The deep, slightly sour taste of Duchy Originals Morello Cherry Preserve makes for a sumptuous, 'adult' trifle. We show you how to make the custard and sponge, but you could buy them from the supermarket if this seems like hard work. You will need 6 tall glasses holding around 200ml (7fl oz) each.

THE SPONGE

see cake recipe on page 115

THE CUSTARD

100g (3½oz) caster sugar

650ml (22fl oz) Duchy Originals or other good organic whole milk

100ml (3½ fl oz) double cream

20g (¾oz) cornflour

1 teaspoon vanilla essence

a scraping of vanilla seeds

125g (4½oz) egg yolk, lightly whipped (about 5 yolks)

THE SYRUP

just over half a jar of Duchy Originals Morello cherry preserve

100ml (3½fl oz) kirsch

THE REMAINING INGREDIENTS

400ml (14fl oz) double cream with 2 tablespoons caster sugar, whipped until thick but not stiff

50g (2oz) hazelnuts, lightly roasted for 5-8 minutes at 180°C/350°F/gas mark 4, then crushed

1 small block good-quality (70% cocoa solids) dark chocolate

Make the sponge following the Victoria Sponge recipe on page 115.

Push the cake out of the tin and leave it on a cake rack to cool. (You will have more sponge than the recipe requires, so freeze the rest for next time).

To make the custard, combine the sugar, milk, cream, cornflour, vanilla essence and vanilla seeds in a heavy-bottomed saucepan. Simmer for 5 minutes, whisking continuously.

Remove the pan from the heat and immediately whisk in the egg yolk.

Return the pan to the hob over very low heat for a minute or two, stirring continuously and the custard is ready. Allow to cool, covered with a layer of greaseproof paper to prevent a skin forming. Store it in the fridge until needed.

To make the syrup: spoon the morello preserve into a saucepan and heat it up gently with the kirsch. Simmer for 5 minutes, give the mixture a stir and leave it to cool.

Now you are in a position to put the trifle together. Slice the sponge into layers about 2cm (¾in) thick, and cut it into circles to fit the trifle glasses. Fill the glasses in the following order: a thin layer of cherry preserve at the bottom, then a layer of custard, then a sponge circle, more cherry, more custard and whipped cream. Finish off with a sprinkling of shaved or grated dark chocolate and the crushed hazelnuts.

Maids of Honour with Almonds and Marmalade

Maids of Honour tarts have been sold in Richmond, Surrey, since 1750, but their pedigree goes back even further. According to legend, Henry VIII discovered the recipe in a locked iron chest in nearby Hampton Court Palace. He gave it to Anne Boleyn, who was then Lady in Waiting to his first wife Catherine of Aragon, and was so delighted with the samples she made for him that he named the cakes in her honour.

Nick, who grew up in Richmond, has adapted the traditional recipe to incorporate marmalade. You will need a 20-22cm (8-9in) non-stick flan tin, about 4cm (1½in) high, with a removable base.

THE PASTRY

1½ large eggs (see below)

200g (7oz) plain flour

75g (3oz) butter

50g (2oz) icing sugar

a couple of drops of vanilla essence

THE FILLING

2 large eggs, plus the whipped half egg left over from the pastry

100g (3½oz) caster sugar

25g (1oz) plain flour

200g (7oz) ground almonds

75g (3oz) Duchy Originals Seville orange marmalade

40ml (1½fl oz) double cream

Start with the pastry. To obtain the requisite half an egg, lightly whip a whole one and divide it into two equal portions. Make sure you keep the other half, as you will be using later as a 'wash' (see below).

Crumble the flour, butter and icing sugar together in a large bowl, using the tips of your fingers. Stir in the eggs and vanilla essence with a large wooden spoon, then gather the pastry together and place it on your kitchen surface. Knead it with the heel of your hand, turning it after each push. Then chill the pastry in the fridge for half an hour or so while you make the filling.

To make the filling, first preheat the oven to 160°C/325°F/gas mark 3. Whip the eggs and sugar together until thick and creamy, using an electric mixer at high speed unless you are prepared for some serious wrist exercise.

Gently fold in the flour, almonds, marmalade and double cream.

Roll the pastry out and use it to line the flan tin, leaving some overlapping the edges, and spoon in the filling.

Bake for 45 minutes. Ten minutes before the end, using a pastry brush, paint the reserved half egg onto the top of the tart as a wash.

Remove the tart from the oven and cut off the overlapping pastry before you push it out of the flan tin.

The tart will keep for a week in an airtight container. It is equally good served warm with vanilla ice cream, or cold with a cup of tea.

Lemon Meringue Pie

Makes 2 tarts which will serve 4–6 people each • Lemon Meringue Pie must be one of the most popular desserts in the world. The key to its success is the textural contrast between crunchy meringue and soft, slippery curd. We've made LMP with various curds and the Duchy Originals version undoubtedly produces the best results. You will need two 20cm (8in) non-stick flan tins with removable bases, about 2.5cm (1in) high.

THE PASTRY

500g (18oz) '00' grade plain flour

175g (6oz) icing sugar

the zest of 1 lemon

250g (9oz) butter, cubed

1 medium egg plus 2 egg yolks

½ teaspoon vanilla essence

THE MERINGUE

4 medium egg whites (see below)

100g (3½oz) caster sugar

75g (3oz) icing sugar

THE FINAL TOUCHES

3 egg yolks (left over from the egg whites)

50ml (2fl oz) double cream

450ml (16fl oz) Duchy Originals lemon curd

To make the pastry, start by sifting the flour and icing sugar into a large bowl. Add the lemon zest, and work in the butter with your fingers until the contents of the bowl are soft and crumbly.

Make a well in the flour, then mix the egg and vanilla together and pour the mixture into the well. Gradually stir in the flour, taking a little more into the centre with each sweep of the spoon.

Loosely press out the pastry and divide it into two balls. Cover them with cling film and transfer them to the fridge, leaving them to rest for half an hour before use.

Preheat the oven to 180ºC/350ºF/gas mark 4.

Roll out each ball of pastry and press it into a tin, leaving a little hanging over the lip. Weigh down the pastry by cutting out a circle of greaseproof paper, placing it on the uncooked pastry and spreading some dried beans or pulses evenly on top.

Bake for 10 minutes, then remove the beans/pulses, trim the overlapping pastry with a sharp knife and cook on for a further 15 minutes.

To make the meringue, whisk the egg whites and icing and caster sugars until stiff peaks are formed.

Now assemble and fill the pies. First, whip the egg yolks and double cream into the lemon curd and pour the mixture into the tart shells. Then top the pies with the whipped egg whites. These are best piped on; alternatively, spoon them on and smooth with a palette knife.

Cook the pies for 40 minutes in an oven at 170ºC/325ºF/gas mark 3. When cooked, the meringue will be crispy and slightly coloured on top and soft in the middle.

Victoria Sponge Filled with Duchy Strawberry Preserve

Sandwich cakes first came into vogue about twenty five years into Queen Victoria's reign. Although it is not known whether the Empress had any particular weakness for this classic afternoon treat, her subjects named it in her honour, just as they called municipal parks throughout the land 'Victoria'.

For this recipe you will need a medium-sized cake tin, 20-22cm (8-9in) in diameter that has been lightly greased with butter and then dusted with flour (turn the tin upside down to shake off any excess).

200g (7oz) unsalted butter

200g (7oz) caster sugar

3 eggs and 3 extra yolks, lightly beaten

200g (7oz) fine plain flour

2 teaspoons baking powder

50ml (2fl oz) double cream

a couple of drops vanilla essence

THE FILLING

200ml (7fl oz) double cream

25g (1oz) caster sugar

125g (4½oz) Duchy Originals strawberry preserve

To make the cake, begin by preheating the oven to 180°C/350°F/ gas mark 4.

Cream the butter and caster sugar together in a large bowl until pale and fluffy, using a spoon or food mixer. The process will be easier if the butter has warmed up to room temperature beforehand.

Slowly add the egg while you carry on beating the butter and caster sugar. If the mixture looks like separating at any point, add a little of the flour.

Sift in the flour and baking powder and mix them in. Finally, fold in the cream and the vanilla essence.

Pour into the cake tin and bake for 45 minutes. Check the cake 10 minutes before the end, as ovens vary in their accuracy.

After the cake has cooled a little, remove it from the tin and leave it to cool on a wire rack.

To make the filling, whip up the double cream with the sugar until thick but not stiff.

Split the cake using a long knife and remove the top.

Spread the preserve directly onto the lower layer of cake and spread the cream directly onto the preserve with a palette knife.

Carefully replace the top layer of cake, and eat it as soon as possible. It will keep for 3 or 4 days in the fridge but is best eaten fresh. If you freeze it immediately, it will keep for a month or two.

Marmalade Cake with Honeycombed Filling

Makes a large cake (16 or more slices) • This indulgent recipe marries tangy Duchy Seville marmalade with a home-made version of the crunchy 'honeycomb' found inside a well-known chocolate bar. Add whipped and soured cream and you have a fantasy of textural contrast. The alchemy involved in making the honeycomb will delight any child almost as much as eating the end product.

EQUIPMENT

silicone sheet (or baking tray lined with greaseproof paper)

4 litre (7 pint), thick-bottomed saucepan

sugar thermometer

cake tin with removable base, 24x8cm (10x3in)

FOR THE HONEYCOMB

75g (3oz) Duchy honey

150ml (¼ pint) liquid glucose

400g (14oz) caster sugar

100ml (3½fl oz) water

15g (¾oz) bicarbonate of soda

FOR THE CAKE

250g (9oz) unsalted butter, at room temperature

250g (9oz) caster sugar

3 large eggs and 1 extra yolk (about 250g/9oz in total)

250g (9oz) flour

2 teaspoons baking powder

50g (2oz) ground almonds

150g (5½oz) Duchy Originals Seville orange marmalade, plus 2 extra tablespoons

100ml (3½fl oz) double cream

50ml (2fl oz) crème fraîche or sour cream

Start with the honeycomb. First loosen the honey and glucose syrup by dipping their containers in warm water, then weigh out into your saucepan. Add the sugar and water and heat gently, stirring until the sugar has dissolved. Gradually raise the temperature of the pan's contents to 150ºC (300ºF). Something dramatic is about to happen.
Carefully sprinkle the bicarbonate of soda into the pan. The contents will fizz up like lava from the underworld, but don't be alarmed - this is what puts the tiny air bubbles into the honeycomb. Stir the mixture to make sure all the powder is incorporated, then pour it out onto your silicone sheet (or baking tray). Leave to set for at least 30 minutes, then break the brittle mass into small pieces. Then take 100g (3½oz) of the honeycomb and blend it in a food processor. Store the remainder in an airtight jar - you will have more than you need - and you are unlikely to regret it.
Preheat the oven to 180ºC/350ºF/gas mark 4. Grease the cake tin with butter, then shake a little flour over it to form a non-stick barrier. Turn the tin upside down and pat it so that any excess flour falls off.
Cream the butter and sugar together in a mixing bowl for 3-5 minutes until pale, light and fluffy. Lightly beat the eggs, and slowly add them to the butter and sugar, mixing them in as you go. If the mixture starts to curdle, beat a little flour into it to bring it back.
Sift the flour and baking powder into the bowl and add the almonds. Mix until the contents are smooth. Fold in the marmalade with 4 swirls of the spoon to ensure that the cake is marbled. Then gently pour the mixture into the cake tin and bake in the oven until cooked and firm (about 50 minutes).
Turn the cake onto a wire rack. When it has cooled, cut it through the middle with a long serrated knife and lift off the top half. Spread the bottom half of the cake with the 2 extra tablespoons of marmalade. Then whip up the honeycomb with the cream and crème fraîche until stiff, and blob it over the marmalade. Replace the top of the cake and leave it to set in a cool place for an hour. Then tuck in...

Wild Strawberry and Raspberry Preserve

Makes about 10 pots of varying sizes • Wild strawberries grow in glades and hummocks, creases, nooks and hedgerows, often in the deepest countryside. They are smaller than their cultivated cousins, with a much more intense flavour, and are a delight for the senses. Unfortunately, wild animals love them too, so human foragers face stiff competition. Raspberries also grow wild, typically in remote regions. We always seem to come across them in hilly areas of Wales and Scotland.

Luckily you don't have to use wild fruit in this recipe; it works well with shop-bought or home-grown raspberries and strawberries, though the end product will not be quite so luxurious. If you do use tame varieties, use British ones in season. A 50/50 mix is ideal for this recipe, but it doesn't matter if you have slightly less of either fruit.

For this recipe you will need a large heavy-bottomed saucepan, a jam thermometer, a jam funnel (or a ladle or jug in its absence), a couple of clean tea cloths and some jam jars. Keep your hands clean, especially when potting off the jam.

3kg (6lb 8oz) hulled strawberries and raspberries

juice of 2 lemons

2.5kg (5lb 8oz) sugar

If the strawberries are large (which they won't be if they are wild), chop them up a bit. Place them in a large saucepan with the lemon juice and whole raspberries and gently boil for an hour or so until the volume has reduced by about 10 per cent.

Add the sugar and continue to boil until setting point is reached (104ºC/220ºF). Heated sugar is temperamental stuff, so you need to be precise about the temperature, hence the need for a thermometer. Remove the jam from the heat, skim off any scum, and leave on the side until a skin has formed on the surface.

While the jam is setting, you need to sterilise your funnel, jam jars and lids. Do this by immersing them in boiling water for 10 minutes.

Place the jars on the tea cloths, then stir the jam and pour it into them, preferably using a funnel. Screw the lids on immediately. As the jam cools, a protective vacuum will form, pulling the lids tightly down.

This jam will keep for at least a year if stored in a cool place.

Organic English Damson Preserve with Rice Pudding

This is a fabulous combination, particularly when you factor in the damson and port sauce. The longer and slower you cook a rice pudding, the better it will be. Use a rectangular Pyrex or ceramic dish with a capacity of at least 1½ litres (2½ pints) and bake the pudding without a lid.

THE RICE PUDDING

75g (3oz) round pudding rice

750ml (1¼ pints) Duchy Originals or other good whole organic milk

100ml (3½fl oz) cream

30g (1oz) butter

a few drops of vanilla essence

1 tablespoon caster sugar

THE DAMSON AND PORT SAUCE

3 large tablespoons Duchy Originals damson preserve

3 large tablespoons port

Mix all the ingredients for the rice pudding together in your dish, and bake in a very low oven (120ºC/250ºF/gas mark ½) for 1 hour. At this point, give the pudding a light stir and return it to the oven for a further 3 hours of slow baking.

At the end of this period, boil up the damson preserve with the port in a small saucepan and serve with the rice pudding.

ROOT VEGETABLE HARVEST

Duchy Originals organic vegetable crisps make the potato variety seem thoroughly passé, both taste-wise and in appearance. They are made with regular varieties of sweet carrots, parsnips and beetroot and are remarkable for their simplicity. The vegetables, many of which are grown at Home Farm, are thinly sliced and hand fried in sunflower oil by a specialist firm in Staffordshire. They are then dusted with sea salt, filled into smart bags and despatched to the shops.

The Home Farm vegetables are grown in six-foot beds and usually planted in three rows. This arrangement allows as much mechanical weeding as possible, which is more efficient and less costly than hand weeding. Some hand weeding, however, is always required. This is done using a bed-weeder. This consists of a frame wide enough to cover three beds of vegetables, with nine 'stretchers' suspended along its breadth a foot or so above the ground. One worker lies on each stretcher, and removes weeds by hand as the tractor makes its stately progress along the beds. Traditional weeding is back-breaking work, but this technique makes it almost luxurious.

The root vegetables are typically grown in sandy soil, which makes them easier to harvest and tastier than average. They are harvested in Autumn using a top-lifting device which pulls them up by the leaves. This minimises damage to the crops and leaves the soil behind. The carrots are particularly fragrant, yielding a herby 'carrot gas' as they are lifted from the soil.

Using the root vegetables to make crisps circumvents the problem of 'outgrading', the process by which supermarkets reject a proportion of vegetables because they do not meet set specifications for size and shape.

The majority of the carrots grown on the farm do pass the outgrading test and are sold to supermarkets. The remainder, apart from those used for the root vegetable crisps, are sold to local schools, as are the bulk of the potatoes. Home Farm also operates a box scheme, delivering to about 140 families within a 10-mile radius of Tetbury. Such schemes are an excellent way to ensure a good supply of organic vegetables and we strongly recommend you to investigate the possibilities in your area.

Toad in the Hole with Mashed Root Vegetables

Makes 8 • The 'toad' in this dish, in case anyone is unsure about this, is actually sausage rather than amphibian. This is an up-market version of a perennial favourite, made with Duchy Originals ale and fresh thyme. Make sure you eat it straight from the oven while the batter is at its crispiest. For this recipe you will need a muffin tin with 12 muffin moulds.

FOR THE TOAD

1 pack of Duchy Selections pork chipolatas (i.e. 8 chipolatas weighing 340g/12oz)

125g (4½oz) plain flour

½ teaspoon salt

ground pepper

2 large eggs

100ml (3½fl oz) Duchy Originals ale

80ml (3fl oz) Duchy Originals milk or other good whole organic milk

olive oil

some sprigs of thyme

FOR THE MASH

4 medium potatoes, each peeled, washed and cut into 4

1 small celeriac, peeled, washed and cut into chunks

4 medium carrots, peeled, washed and roughly sliced

a large knob of butter

a splash of double cream

a fistful of roughly chopped flat leaf parsley

salt and freshly ground black pepper

Preheat the oven to 180ºC/350ºF/gas mark 4 and bake the chipolatas for 15 minutes until nicely browned. Remove from the oven and reserve.

Turn the heat up to 220ºC/425ºF/gas mark 7, pending the arrival of the assembled toad in the hole.

To make the mashed root vegetables, boil the potato, celeriac and carrot together for about 30 minutes until nice and soft.

Mix the flour with the salt and a little ground pepper in a large bowl. Stir in the eggs, then slowly whisk in the beer and milk.

Take the muffin tin and pour a dribble of olive oil into each mould. Place the tin in the oven for 5 minutes until the oil is smoking hot. Remove it carefully and immediately distribute the batter equally into the muffin moulds.

Push half a chipolata into each 'toad' and sprinkle with a sprig or two of thyme, followed by a grind of black pepper.

Bake for 15 minutes until fully risen and irresistible.

Pour off the water and mash in the pan along with the butter, cream, parsley, salt and pepper. Serve with the toad in the hole and lashings of Duchy Originals Poultry Gravy or make your own.

100g (3½oz) Duchy Originals back bacon or streaky bacon, cut into small lardons

1 medium onion, roughly chopped

2 sticks of celery, roughly chopped

2 medium carrots, peeled and roughly sliced

2 garlic cloves, finely chopped

350g (12oz) brown cap mushrooms (Portobello or chestnut), roughly sliced

30g (1oz) butter

1.1 litres (1¾ pints) chicken stock (or use the same amount of water and 2 teaspoons organic vegetable bouillon)

350g (12oz) peeled and diced potatoes

a handful of dried porcini mushrooms (if they look dirty, soak them in a little hot water before you use them).

1 teaspoon chopped fresh thyme

100ml (3½fl oz) double cream

salt and freshly ground pepper

a good fistful of roughly chopped flat leaf parsley

Wild Mushroom and Bacon Soup

Serves 4 • This is a simple soup to make, but very impressive. Try to make sure you use fresh chicken stock - it boosts the flavour no end when it combines with the mushrooms and bacon.

Fry the bacon over medium heat in the same saucepan you will use to cook the soup. Reserve.
Using the same pan, fry the onion, celery, carrots, garlic and mushrooms in the butter for around 15 minutes over moderate heat with the lid on, stirring occasionally.

Pour in the stock and add the potatoes, porcini mushrooms (including the soaking liquid which contains lots of flavour) and thyme. Simmer for at least 20 minutes until the potatoes are soft.
Blend the soup until smooth, then add the cream. Season with salt and pepper, then stir in the bacon and flat leaf parsley.
Serve with toasted Duchy Originals bread.

Roasted Carrot with Beetroot, Goat's Cheese and Baked Almonds

Serves 4 • This salad is best served warm. It looks particularly good if you use a bi-coloured variety of beetroot called 'Chioggia', pictured on page 164, but don't worry if you can't track any down.

400g (14oz) small whole carrots, trimmed and cleaned

olive oil

a sprig or two of fresh thyme, chopped

5 fresh sage leaves, chopped

1 tablespoon chopped flat leaf parsley

a couple of fistfuls of flaked almonds

3 medium beetroot

75g (3oz) goat's cheese (mild or mature, depending on your preference), crumbled

Duchy Originals honey and mustard vinaigrette

Preheat the oven to 200ºC/400ºF/gas mark 6.

Roast the carrots for 30 minutes in a small tin with a little olive oil and salt and pepper.

For the last 5 minutes of the roasting period, put the almonds (in another roasting tray) in the oven, cook until golden brown and reserve. As soon as you take them out of the oven, put them in a large bowl and toss them with the thyme, sage and parsley.

Meanwhile, boil the beetroot for 30 minutes. Allow to cool enough for you to peel the skin, and then slice.

Add the beetroot and goat's cheese to the carrot mixture, and sprinkle the almonds on top. Finally, dress the salad with the vinaigrette and serve it with warmed Duchy Originals Vintage Cheddar Cheese Bread.

As a variation, try making this salad with cheddar instead of goat's cheese.

Baked Home Farm Potatoes with Field Mushroom Sauce

Serves 2–3 • For this quick, easy dish, use the biggest field mushrooms you can find. If you pick them yourself, make sure you get them positively identified by someone who knows what they are doing. Otherwise, farmed ones are available in the shops year round.

2 or 3 medium baking potatoes (200-250g/7-9oz each)

a head of garlic

4 large field mushrooms (about 200g/7oz), sliced

unsalted butter

1 heaped teaspoon chopped thyme

4 sage leaves, chopped

100g (3½oz) brie, rind removed

1 heaped tablespoon crème fraîche

freshly grated nutmeg

salt and pepper

olive oil

Preheat the oven to 220ºC/425ºF/gas mark 7.

Wash the potatoes and scrub the skins, pricking them a few times to stop them splitting during cooking. Bake for an hour or so until the skins are crisp. For the last 20-25 minutes, add the garlic head. Prepare it by cutting its top off, seasoning with a little salt, pepper and olive oil and wrapping it in tin foil.

Remove the potatoes and garlic from the oven, unwrapping the latter and leaving it to cool for a few minutes to save your fingers.

Fry the mushrooms with a large piece of butter until cooked, then add the thyme and sage.

Take the garlic in your hand and squeeze the soft paste into the pan. We use the whole head, but you don't have to. Cook over moderate heat for another couple of minutes, stirring constantly. Add the brie, crème fraîche and about a quarter of a grated nutmeg, and stir over low heat until the cheese has melted.

Season with salt and pepper, then cut the potatoes open, pour the sauce over/into them and serve.

Ham and Organic Potatoes Baked with Cheddar Cheese

Serves 4 • This dish is easy to make, but enormously satisfying on a cold autumnal day. You will need a well-greased oven dish with dimensions of approximately 18 x 25 x 6cm (7 x 10 x 2½in).

1kg (2¼lb) medium potatoes, cut into slices about 1cm (½in) thick

300g (10½oz) cheddar cheese, grated

200ml (7fl oz) crème fraîche or sour cream

a small bunch of spring onions, chopped

a handful of flat leaf parsley, chopped

salt and freshly ground black pepper

140g (5oz) Duchy Selections ham, roughly chopped

freshly grated nutmeg

Preheat the oven to 200ºC/400ºF/gas mark 6 and while it is warming up, boil the potato slices in a saucepan for 12-15 minutes.

Mix the cheddar cheese, crème fraîche, spring onions, flat leaf parsley, a little salt and pepper and most of the ham (leaving a bit aside for the topping) in a large bowl.

Line the bottom of your baking dish with a single layer of sliced potatoes. Spoon about half the cheese mix on top, then add another layer of potatoes, and finally the rest of the mix.

Sprinkle with the rest of the ham and a generous dusting of grated nutmeg.

Bake for 20 minutes until the dish is brown and crispy on top.

Chicken Roasted with Shallots and Duchy Originals Poultry Gravy

Serves 4 • Nick was involved in developing the Duchy Originals Poultry Gravy, so he knows exactly how good it is. It is made with fresh stock, white wine and sage, and using it in this recipe will save you a lot of work.

There is a lot to be said for spatchcocking (flattening) your chicken before you roast it. Spatchcocked chickens cook more quickly than regular birds; if you use one, you can make this dish from scratch in 1½ hours. Either ask your butcher to spatchcock the chicken, which he will do in a split second, or have a go yourself. To do this, turn the bird breast side up with the wings closest to you. Taking a sharp knife or pair of poultry shears, make an incision into the sternum and cut away from you while you hold the chicken by the drumsticks. Cut all the way to the end of the chicken, then flatten it with your hands. You can make sure it stays flat by passing a couple of kebab sticks through the flesh.

1 medium organic chicken, about 1.5kg (3lb 5oz)

3 garlic cloves, cut into 2 or 3 pieces

12 medium shallots, peeled

salt and pepper

olive oil

a glass of white wine

a pot of Duchy Originals poultry gravy

100ml (3½fl oz) water

Preheat the oven to 220ºC/425ºF/gas mark 7.

Make a few slits in the chicken skin and strategically intersperse the garlic pieces by pushing them underneath with your finger.

Season the chicken and shallots with salt and pepper and baste with a drop of olive oil.

Place the chicken in a baking dish, surround it with the shallots and pour in the white wine.

Roast for 15 minutes, then turn the heat down to 180ºC/350ºF/gas mark 4 and cook for another hour.

When the chicken is cooked, remove the bird and the shallots and pour the Duchy gravy into the baking tin with the water. Gently heat the tin on the stove top, scraping all the chicken bits that have adhered to it back into the gravy.

Serve the chicken and shallots with this delicious gravy, accompanied by roast potatoes and runner beans.

Chicken and Bacon Casserole with Duchy Originals Poultry Gravy

Serves 4 • This warming casserole is topped with a crispy breadcrumb crust, or 'streusel'. You can use white chicken meat if you prefer, but we find legs have more flavour.

THE CASSEROLE

4 large pieces of chicken (whole breasts, or legs and thighs)

salt and pepper

25g (1oz) butter

4 slices of Duchy Originals back bacon, roughly sliced

1 medium onion, sliced

150ml (¼ pint) white wine

a pot of Duchy Originals poultry gravy

100ml (3½fl oz) water

4 medium potatoes, thinly sliced

3 medium leeks, trimmed and roughly chopped

4 fresh sage leaves, chopped

grated nutmeg

THE STREUSEL

50g (2oz) fresh breadcrumbs (to make these, pulse fresh white bread in the food processor until crumbed)

20g (¾oz) butter

a small bunch of chives, chopped

a pinch of salt

To make the streusel, place all ingredients in a bowl and rub them together with your fingers.

Preheat the oven to 180ºC/350ºF/gas mark 4.

Season the chicken pieces with a little salt and pepper and fry in the butter over moderate heat until browned (about 5 minutes). Reserve.

Using the same pan, fry the bacon and onion over moderate heat until soft (5-8 minutes).

Add the white wine, the Duchy Originals poultry gravy and the water.

Place the potatoes in a layer at the bottom of the casserole dish, then add the chicken. Push the leeks down between the pieces of chicken and pour the sauce evenly over the top. Season with the salt, pepper, sage and nutmeg.

Cover the dish and bake for 2 hours.

Uncover the dish and sprinkle the streusel on top. Turn the oven up to 220ºC/425ºF/gas mark 7 and bake for a further 10 minutes until golden brown.

Serve with steamed runner beans and carrots.

Organic Potato Crisps with Sage, Rosemary and Thyme

Duchy Originals, of course, make delightful root vegetable crisps, but here we show you how to make a traditional potato version. You can turn any variety of potato into crisps, but red organic potatoes yield particularly good results. Young specimens at the beginning of the season produce light-coloured crisps because their sugar level is low. After they go into storage, the sugar level increases, so as the season progresses you will end up with darker, more caramelised crisps.

Rather a lot of oil is left on the finished crisps, and this is what makes them so tasty. Try experimenting with different types of potato. Some will be more robust than others when cooked. We prefer a light powdery bite. The seasoning for the crisps should be ground down quite fine for an even coating.

These crisps can be stored in an airtight container for a month or two if you don't open the lid.

For this recipe you will need a deep-fat fryer or pan and a thermometer. A kitchen mandolin will also come in handy. Ours slices potatoes beautifully, producing crisps about 1mm thick.

organic sunflower oil

potatoes, cleaned but not peeled

1 teaspoon dry sage

1 teaspoon dry rosemary

1 teaspoon dry thyme

sea salt and freshly ground black pepper

Heat the oil to 140ºC (280ºF) checking the temperature with your thermometer.

Thinly slice the potatoes with a mandolin. Fry them in small batches, no more than 15 at a time. They will fry vigorously at first and then slow down. Only remove them from the pan when they have completely stopped bubbling, otherwise they may go soft. Extract them with a slotted implement, place them on kitchen paper and pat them dry. Then transfer them to an airtight container.

Crush the sage, rosemary, thyme, pepper and 1½ teaspoons salt as finely as possible using a pestle and mortar or a spice grinder.

Take a few pinches of this mix and sprinkle onto the crisps. Gently move them around and turn them over to ensure an even distribution. When you are happy with the level of seasoning, you can store the rest for a future batch, or use it to rub on meat prior to cooking.

ALE

After the Plumage Archer barley grown at Home Farm is harvested in August or September, it is cleaned and dried to keep the seed dormant. Then it is sent via a malting house to the Wychwood Brewery in the market town of Witney, Oxfordshire to be brewed into the Duchy Originals range of ales. The brewery occupies the town's nineteenth-century Eagle Maltings, a higgledy-piggledy collection of attractive Cotswold stone buildings tucked away off the high street. The site is easy enough to find, however, as it radiates a powerful aroma of malt.

Jeremy Moss, the Head Brewer, is a friendly and patient man, well used to explaining the mechanics of ale production to those whose experience begins and ends in the pub. He begins by outlining the malting process. First, the barley is soaked in cold water and spread out on large trays. It is then left to germinate, which releases the starch stored inside the seed. After five days, the malted barley, as it is now called, is roasted in a kiln to halt its growth. Most of the barley used in the Duchy Originals ales is dry-kilned, which produces a pale malt with a bready taste. Ten per cent, however, has a little water added beforehand. When kilned, this becomes crystal malt, which imparts a toffee/caramel-like flavour to the beers. Both kinds of malt are then transferred to a huge silo. Then, on the day prior to brewing, they are crushed into a coarse powder called grist, which is the origin of the expression 'grist to the mill'.

Above Jeremy Moss, head brewer. **Opposite, main photograph** The 'copper'
in Wychwood Brewery. **Far right, top** Jeremy, peering into a fermentation vat.
Far right, bottom The head on fermenting ale.

Brewing proper begins when the grist is mixed with a copious quantity
of hot water, or 'liquor' as it is perversely known in the trade. Mark,
the worker responsible, judges how much malt to add by eye, using
a torch to peer into the container. The liquid is then pumped into a
gigantic barrel called a mash tun at a temperature of 66ºC (150ºF).
The heat causes the starch in the malted barley to dissolve,
whereupon it is converted to sugar by enzymes present in the malt.
After an hour, the sweetened liquid or 'wort' is drawn off, and hot
water is sprayed into the tun to extract any remaining sugar from the
mash in a process known as 'sparging'. Brewing evidently demands
not only technical expertise, but mastery of an entire vocabulary.

After it has left the mash tun, the wort is piped into the adjacent
copper kettle, which has a handsome top dating from around 1900. At
this point, organic hops are added in pellet form, and the wort is
boiled for an hour. It then passes into a separator, where it whirls
around gently, looking not unlike loose leaf tea. The rotary motion

causes the liquid and solid components to separate, the latter being
deposited as a cone in the middle of the vessel. Along with the residue
from the mash tun, they are sold as nutritious animal feed. Yeast is
then added to the hop-enriched wort, which is cooled to 16ºC (60ºF)
and transferred to the fermentation tanks. It remains in the tanks for
three to four days, developing a spectacular foamy head as the yeast
breaks down the sugar into alcohol and carbon dioxide.

Once fermented, the young ale is piped into road tankers and
cooled to -1ºC (30ºF). It is then driven to Burton-on-Trent in the
Potteries, where it is filtered through ceramic earth to remove any
remaining impurities. Finally, it is bottled, pasteurised and passed on
to the distributors.

By now we are ready for a drink. We repair to the company
boardroom, where bottles of all three ales brewed on the site for
Duchy Originals await us. Sadly, it is a bit early in the day for beer, so
we settle for tea while Jeremy eulogises the qualities of the Duchy
products. The strongest is the Winter Ale, a rich, dark beer with an
alcohol content of 6.2 per cent. The Original Ale comes next in terms
of strength (5 per cent) and top in terms of sales. It is ruby coloured,
with a slightly bitter, toffee-ish taste. Finally, there is the fragrant
Summer Ale, pale and light with an alcohol content of 4.7 per cent. To
give it a summery zing, a little yeast is added at the bottling stage to
encourage further fermentation.

Johnny has always been a lager man, but by the time we leave the
brewery his allegiance has been deeply shaken. Things come to a
head when Percy, his wife, makes a delicious Welsh Rarebit
incorporating some of the Duchy Winter Ale and joyfully knocks back
the rest of the bottle. Johnny cracks, and now drinks little else.

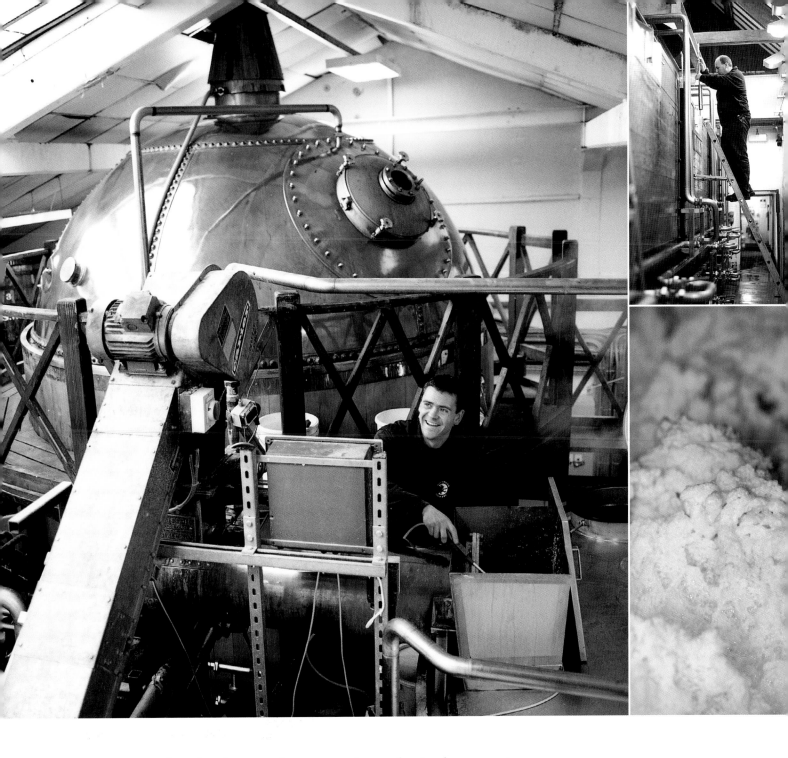

Brewing evidently demands not only technical expertise,

but mastery of an entire vocabulary.

Beef Stew with Duchy Originals Ale and Horseradish Dumplings

Serves 4–6 • Here is a rich, addictive stew to warm the cockles of your heart. It is a thoroughly British alternative to boeuf bourguignon and the horseradish dumplings pack quite a punch.

THE STEW

16 small shallots, peeled

olive oil

800g (1lb 10oz) diced beef

25g (1oz) butter

200g (7oz) chestnut mushrooms, sliced

150g (5½oz) fresh tomatoes, chopped

400ml (14fl oz) Duchy Originals ale

3 bay leaves

1 teaspoon chopped fresh thyme

THE DUMPLINGS

120g (4½oz) shredded suet

250g (9oz) plain flour

½ teaspoon salt

1½ teaspoons baking powder

40g (1½oz) finely grated horseradish – to avoid an emotional experience, grate it wearing a swimming mask or under an extractor hood

1 teaspoon mustard powder

To make the stew, begin by gently frying the whole shallots in a little olive oil in a large pan until browned. Remove them from the pan and reserve.

Splash a little more olive oil into the pan and turn the heat right up. Hard fry the beef in small batches until browned and reserve.

Place the butter in the pan, without an intervening wash, and fry off the mushrooms. Then add the tomatoes and ale and reintroduce the beef and shallots. Add the bay leaves and thyme and simmer for 2 hours, stirring occasionally. You may need to top up with a little water.

To make the dumplings, first rub the suet into the flour, salt and baking powder in a large bowl. Add the horseradish and mustard powder, and gradually mix in water until you have a firmish dough. Separate the dough into 12 walnut-sized dumplings.

To finish off the stew, preheat the oven to 180ºC/350ºF/gas mark 4. Pour the hot stew into a casserole dish, making sure there is enough liquid in it. If you are uncertain, add a little water.

Stud the dumplings into the stew, leaving a space between them to give them room to rise. Cover the casserole dish with its lid or tin foil, and bake for 30 minutes. Then take off the lid, turn up the heat to 220ºC/425ºF/gas mark 7, and cook for another 10 minutes to brown the dumplings.

Eat immediately with lots of beer.

Game Pie

This recipe makes eight individual pies, and so is perfect if you are expecting friends or family. The gamey tastes of the pheasant and venison are brought out by the red wine, fennel and porcini mushrooms. These pies are excellent cold as well as hot, but don't eat them straight out of the fridge or you'll lose some of the flavours.

You need a whole boned pheasant for this recipe. If you can do this yourself, so much the better; if not, ask your butcher to do it.

THE STOCK

bones from 1 medium pheasant (reserve the breast and thigh meat for the filling)

1 stick of celery

1 medium carrot

1 small onion

olive oil

salt and freshly ground black pepper

a glass of red wine

a few slices of dried porcini mushrooms

2 bay leaves

4 cloves

THE FILLING

the meat from 1 boned pheasant, diced

250g (9oz) venison haunch steak, diced

olive oil

40g (1½oz) smoked pancetta or Duchy Originals streaky bacon, finely diced

30g (1oz) unsalted butter

1 medium carrot, diced

2 medium shallots, diced

½ a fennel bulb, diced

1 heaped tablespoon plain flour

400ml (14fl oz) game stock

THE PASTRY

see Old English pastry recipe on page 204

THE EGG GLAZE

1 egg, lightly whipped

First make the stock. Take a small baking dish and roast the pheasant bones for 20 minutes at 220ºC/425ºF/gas mark 7 with the celery, carrot and onion. Baste with a drop of olive oil and a touch of salt and pepper.

Place the contents in a medium saucepan. Scrape out the tasty bits which have adhered to the baking dish with a little boiling water and pour this into the saucepan too.

Add a glass of red wine, the porcini mushrooms, bay leaves and cloves. Top up with water until it almost reaches the top of the bones. **Simmer** for a couple of hours, but don't add any more water. As a guide, you are looking to end up with about 400ml (14fl oz) of stock.

Now make the filling. Fry off the pheasant and venison in a drop of olive oil over quite a fierce heat until browned. Add the diced pancetta and fry on for a minute or two.

Turn down the heat, add the butter, carrot, shallots and fennel and gently fry for another 8-10 minutes.

Spoon in the flour and mix it in until you can't see it anymore. Then pour in a little of the warm game stock and stir it in. The mixture will become thick and gluey. Pour in a little more game stock, stir it in and then add and stir in the rest of the stock.

Simmer for 15 minutes, then test the pie filling for seasoning, adding some more if necessary. Leave the filling to cool while you make the pastry, following the recipe on page 204.

Take the dough out of the fridge and divide into 8 portions (each will weigh about 80g/3oz) . Roll each portion into a ball.

Now put the pies together. First, preheat the oven to 200ºC/400ºF/gas mark 6. Then take each ball of dough and roll it out into a square about 15 x 15cm (6 x 6in). Place 80-100g (3-3½oz) of pie filling in the middle of each square, then pull up the diagonally opposing corners of the pastry so that they meet in the middle and press together. Repeat with the other corners, then press the 'seams' together.

Place the pies on a greased baking sheet or silicone sheet and use a pastry brush to paint them with the egg wash.

Bake for 10 minutes, then turn down the heat to 180ºC/350ºF/gas mark 4 and cook for another 25-30 minutes until golden brown.

Pigeon Breast With Smoked Streaky Bacon and Port

Serves 2 • Wood pigeon is frequently available at good butchers and farmers' markets. The breasts are lean and should never be overdone. This recipe takes no more than 10 minutes to cook and your guest(s) will be highly impressed.

2 pigeon breast fillets

salt and freshly ground pepper

olive oil

25g (1oz) Duchy Originals streaky bacon or smoked pancetta, finely diced

50ml (2fl oz) port

a couple of sprigs of thyme, chopped

25g (1oz) butter

Lightly score the pigeon breasts on the skin side with a tight crisscross pattern, and season with salt and pepper.
Heat up a small frying pan with a smidgeon of olive oil and gently fry the breasts for around 4 minutes on each side (skin side down first).
Remove the pigeon breasts and lightly cover them to keep them warm. Using the same pan, fry the bacon or pancetta over medium heat for 4 minutes, stirring frequently. Add the port and thyme and bring to the boil. Then add the butter and reduce the liquid for a minute or two. Check for seasoning, and serve with the pigeon breast.
This dish looks and tastes particularly good with the breasts propped up on a small nest of shredded Savoy cabbage.

Potted Venison

Makes one big pot • This is a luxurious indulgence. It is extremely rich and almost unnervingly fatty, but the pay off is sublime taste and texture. Spread it on warm toast whenever you need a lift.

500g (18oz) venison fillet, cut into large chunks

250ml (9fl oz) chicken stock

200ml (7fl oz) port

3 cloves

10 black peppercorns

2 cardamom pods

1 star anise

150ml (¼ pint) goose fat

Simmer all the ingredients apart from the goose fat together for at least 2 hours, then remove the venison and leave it to cool.
Strain off the stock and return the pan to the stove. Slowly reduce until you are left with about 50ml (2fl oz) of intense concentrate.
While the stock is reducing, shred the venison into strands. Either use your clean fingers or a couple of forks.
Add the shredded venison to the stock, together with the goose fat. Simmer for 5 minutes or so and pour into an earthenware pot.
Press the venison down so that the goose fat forms a layer above the meat. Cover tightly and set in the fridge.
The potted venison will keep for around 10 days before you have broken the fatty seal, but after you have broken it consume within 5 days.

HERRING & MACKEREL

Duchy Originals is concerned, as we all should be, about declining fish stocks. Since 2002, the company has worked closely with the Marine Stewardship Council (MSC) to help support sustainable fisheries and publicise the cause. The MSC seeks not only to protect fish populations but also the marine environment and the livelihoods of traditional fishing communities.

The first fruits of the partnership are two delectable patés sold under the Duchy Selections label. The first to be launched was the gooseberry and cornish mackerel paté, made with fish caught by handline off the Cornish peninsula. Then, in 2004, a kipper and lemon paté was introduced, made with Thames Estuary herring (*Clupea harengus*), a species unique to England's Eastern coastal waters. Smaller than Atlantic herring and with one fewer vertebra, they can only be legally fished within a six-mile zone around the Thames, Blackwater and Colne estuaries. There is an embargo on fishing for them during their spawning season in March and April,

and the herring are caught with drift nets with a sufficiently wide mesh to allow immature fish to swim through. The indiscriminate practice of trawling is strictly forbidden. Most of the herring are landed in West Mersea. Those used for the Duchy Selections paté are kippered locally by a local specialist smokery, Ken Green Fish Merchants, in Clacton, Essex.

One drizzly Autumn day, Nick and Jonathan the photographer travel to Newlyn in Cornwall to see what sustainable fishing is all about. The mackerel boats depart before dawn, so the following morning they are in the Fisherman's Mission Café an hour before sunrise to meet local fisherman John Stevens. John is blond, rugged and good natured, with a deep tan born of a life spent out in the elements. He loves his work, which is as well given the long hours, and asks little from his time on shore beyond a regular curry with his mates.

As we revive ourselves with mugs of tea, John gives us an overview of the local mackerel fishery. The season runs from May to February, and the fish are caught by handline. He keeps his boat relatively close to the shore, and alternates between the Penzance and St Ives sides of the peninsula. Catches are somewhat archaically weighed in stone, with 30 stone (190kg/420lb) considered a good day's haul.

Previous pages John Stevens in his boat. **Left** The mackerel fishing boats are surprisingly small. **Top row** Fish crates at Newlyn market. **Bottom row** A mackerel boat at sea and some of the catch.

The fishing boats go out to sea en masse, bobbing about like
a flotilla of brightly coloured bathtubs, which they
resemble in size.

Thus briefed, we make our way along the quayside to John's boat, a Plymouth Pilot named the *Janet Ann*. He raises a moistened finger and mutters 'when the wind is in the East, the fish are at their least'. Fortunately, the easterly breeze is very gentle this morning. When we board the *Janet Ann*, John shows us his fishing equipment, which consists of an electronic fish-finder, a radio, a handline with 40 feathered hooks, a selection of plastic boxes and nothing else. We are amazed by the simplicity.

The fishing boats go out to sea en masse, bobbing about like a flotilla of brightly coloured bathtubs, which they resemble in size. Before long, John detects a shoal on the fish-finder. A split second later, he hauls up the handline and shakes thirty glistening mackerel onto the deck. There is a pandemonium of thrashing fish. Before the boat has had time to pass through the shoal, John has lowered the heavily weighted line again and pulled up another load. He then sorts through the fish, throwing any shorter than 20cm (8in) back into the sea to comply with MSC regulations, and moves on. There is then a long quiet spell, followed by another bout of frantic activity, and the pattern repeats itself throughout the morning.

When we return to shore, we accompany the catch to the market in Newlyn, where the fish are sorted into grades and weighed and tagged by MSC representatives. Marine scientists wander around the market seeking to establish quotas. They pay close attention to logbooks, egg counts and otoliths, which are age-revealing growth rings in the fish's ears. The mackerel are then refrigerated and auctioned whole to professional fish buyers. It is from these middlemen that Duchy Originals purchase the fish for their mackerel and gooseberry paté.

Freshly caught mackerel are incomparably better than the older specimens typically sold in fishmongers, and on the way back to London Nick cannot resist an impromptu beach barbecue. He has had the foresight to bring his portable hot smoker (see overleaf), which he sets up in a jiffy. Then he produces a range of essential seasonings from his voluminous pockets - salt, pepper, fresh thyme and ground paprika - and uses them to coat and stuff the fish. To speed up the cooking process, he covers the smoker with bladderwrack and kelp seaweed so that the mackerel effectively 'smoke roasts'. They are ready within half an hour and are quite exquisite.

Smoking is an ancient technique that both preserves food and infuses it with delicious, savoury flavours. Buying smoked fish, however, can be a bit of a minefield. There are two main reasons for this. First, the quality of commercially smoked foods varies wildly, depending on whether the manufacturers are genuinely working to enhance their raw materials, or unscrupulously cutting corners to secure the premium prices smoked products command. Some foods sold as 'smoked', for instance, are really nothing of the kind, having simply been immersed in what the industry calls 'liquid smoke'. Second, there is a crucial distinction between cold smoking and hot smoking, and it is important to understand the difference.

With these considerations in mind, we thought we'd explain the nomenclature and give you a few tips about what to look for when buying smoked fish. You may also want to try smoking at home – it is great fun – so we wanted to give you some idea of where to start.

First, the terminology. Hot smoking both smokes and cooks the food, while cold smoking just smokes it. Some cold-smoked fish is best eaten 'raw' – smoked salmon is a prime example – and some needs to be cooked, for example the kipper. As a further complication, some fish, such as salmon, is sold in both hot- and cold-smoked forms. Other things being equal, cold-smoked varieties will have a deep but more delicate flavour and hot-smoked ones will have a cooked texture and a stronger but less subtle smokiness.

As usual, we would advise you to buy smoked fish with an MSC (Marine Stewardship Council) label, or other evidence that it has been sourced from sustainable fisheries. Check whether the fish has been hot or cold smoked and avoid products with too many additives (particularly the dreaded 'liquid smoke'). If the food is stuffed with preservatives, you have to ask why, given that smoking is a preservative in itself.

If you want to try smoking at home, our first advice is to get a good book on the subject. There is plenty of information on both cold and hot smoking in Nick and Johnny's book, *Preserved*. Another option is smoke roasting, which cooks food at temperatures higher than those employed in hot smoking, but still imparts a delicious smokiness. This is the technique Nick used for the mackerel beach barbecue pictured opposite and described on page 145.

Mackerel Baked with Sage and Duchy Bacon

Serves 4 as a starter or 2 as a main course • It is one of Nature's happy accidents that the tastes of mackerel and bacon combine to their mutual benefit. The reputation of mackerel sometimes suffers unfairly because it is often sold in a sad state. Make sure you buy firm, shiny fish with bulging, glistening eyes. Ask your fishmonger to fillet two mackerel of your choice into four pieces each. He will do this by cutting the mackerel into two fillets, then cutting each fillet into two lengthways either side of the pin bones. This will leave you with 8 long fillets.

2 very fresh mackerel cut into 8 fillets

16 sage leaves

8 slices of Duchy Originals streaky bacon

salt and pepper

olive oil

Preheat the oven to 220°C/425°F/gas mark 7.
Place the mackerel fillets on a baking tray, skin side up. Plaster 2 sage leaves onto each one, then wrap streaky bacon around it. A sage leaf should protrude from each side of the wrapped bacon.
Season with salt, pepper and brush on a little olive oil. Bake in the oven for a maximum of 15 minutes until the skin and bacon are crispy brown.
This dish is delicious served with spinach and mashed potato.

Smoked Mackerel Risotto

Serves 4 • Some risottos are comfortingly bland, but this one is comfortingly tasty. If you have a risotto pan, the thick bottom and good heat distribution will work to your advantage, but don't worry if you haven't got one. You can use a high-sided frying pan or even a wok.

Risotto should be served al dente (with a little bite). When you pile it on a plate, the mound should gradually subside.

2 medium shallots, chopped

2 garlic cloves, chopped

2 teaspoons black mustard seeds

1 tablespoon butter

250g (9oz) risotto rice

½ glass of white wine

4 cloves

450ml (16fl oz) hot chicken stock

250g (9oz) smoked mackerel, skinned, boned and roughly teased apart

150g (5½oz) spinach, cleaned and roughly chopped

100ml (3½fl oz) crème fraîche

salt and pepper

nutmeg

12 quail's eggs, hard-boiled (cover in water, bring to the boil, then leave to cool)

Fry the shallots, garlic and mustard seeds in the butter for a minute or two, over moderate heat. Add the rice and continue to fry, stirring constantly.

After a few minutes add the wine, cloves and stock, and turn the heat down. Gradually, the rice will start to soak up the stock. As the risotto dries out, you may want to add a little hot water or some more stock.

When the rice is almost cooked (test by tasting it), gently stir in the mackerel, spinach, crème fraîche, salt and pepper and grate a little nutmeg on top.

Serve garnished with the quail's eggs.

Soused Mackerel

Serves 4 as a starter • Sousing is a traditional technique somewhere between pickling and poaching. It works particularly well for oily fish such as mackerel and herring. When we got back from our fishing trip in Cornwall, we smoked some of our mackerel and soused the rest, because after this delicate process they can be stored for in the fridge for up to 7 days.

Ask your fishmonger to fillet 2 good, medium-sized mackerel into 4 pieces in the manner described in the mackerel, bacon and sage recipe on page 148. You will also need some cocktail sticks and a lidded saucepan that can go in the oven.

8 very fresh mackerel fillets

2 medium shallots, peeled and thinly sliced

10 black peppercorns

4 cloves

½ teaspoon salt

1 teaspoon sugar

150ml (¼ pint) white wine vinegar

100ml (3½fl oz) white wine

100ml (3½fl oz) water

a couple of sprigs of tarragon (alternatively use tarragon vinegar)

1 bay leaf

Roll a fillet of mackerel around 2 or 3 slices of shallot with the skin on the outside, and fix with a cocktail stick, piercing the fish through the middle and out the other side.

Repeat with the rest of the fillets and tightly pack them in a single layer at the bottom of the saucepan. If there is excess space, use a smaller pan.

Add the rest of the ingredients to the pan including any extra slices of shallot.

Preheat the oven to 120ºC/250ºF/gas mark ½. Meanwhile, bring the mackerel almost to boiling point on your stove top, then immediately take the pan off the heat and place it in the oven with the lid on.

Remove the mackerel after 45 minutes and leave them to cool in the pan with the lid on. Then transfer them to an airtight container and store in the fridge until you feel peckish.

This dish should be eaten cold, and is superb with beetroot salad and hunks of bread.

ALASKAN SMOKED SALMON

The fish used for the Duchy Selections Smoked Salmon are wild, line-caught Coho Salmon (*Oncorhynchus kisutch*) from the icy waters of Alaska. Like the mackerel and herring used for the patés, they are sourced from sustainable fisheries certified by the Marine Stewardship Council (see page 141). The Coho is one of five locally caught subspecies approved by the Council, the others being Sockeye, Pink, Chum and Chinook. It has a rich, meaty flavour with echoes of shellfish, and is particularly appropriate for smoking due to its high fat content and deep red colour.

The Coho are landed between July and September, during the brief window when the Alaskan seas are free of ice. The salmon are bled and gutted on the spot and then frozen. To ensure consistency of the end product, Duchy Originals only select medium-sized fish and these are subsequently shipped to Scotland. They are smoked in the Spey Valley by Strathaird Salmon, a firm founded by Ian Anderson, the lead singer of the rock band Jethro Tull.

When the fish are about to be smoked, they are removed from storage and carefully 'tempered' (defrosted) to avoid damage to their flesh. They are then split and the spines are removed. Next, the halved fish are dry cured for 21 hours in a mixture of sea salt, Demerara sugar and Duchy Selections Heather Honey (see page 89). At the end of this period, the cure is washed off and the salmon are left for a while to dry. They are then hung on racks and transferred to a smoking kiln that has been in operation since 1888. Here, they are cold smoked for between 20 and 24 hours with hazel chippings from the Duchy of Cornwall's woodland in Herefordshire (see page 40), plus a few whisky barrel oak shavings for extra flavour. They are then left to mature for 48 hours, which allows the smoky residues to distribute themselves evenly through the flesh. Finally, the salmon fillets are trimmed, cut into traditional, thick 'D'-shaped slices and packaged.

There is a fine recipe for smoked salmon fish cakes overleaf, but there is little to beat eating the fish in the traditional manner, namely on good brown bread and butter with a squeeze of lemon juice. Many people grind a little black pepper on top, but we prefer a sprinkling of fiery cayenne pepper. Its heat brings out the delicate flavour of the smoked salmon perfectly.

Smoked Salmon Fish Cakes

Serves 4 • Aside from being very tasty, these cakes have the advantage of being made from fish caught in a sustainable manner. It's good to give the poor, over-fished cod a break.

THE CAKES

500g (18oz) new potatoes, boiled for 30 minutes until slightly overcooked

200g (7oz) Duchy Selections Smoked Salmon

3 spring onions, chopped

25g (1oz) butter

a good handful of chopped flat leaved parsley

1 large egg

salt and pepper

fresh white breadcrumbs, made from 2-3 slices of bread, pulsed quickly in a food processor

olive oil or butter for frying

THE DIPPING SAUCE

small tub (142ml/5fl oz) sour cream

a small bunch of chopped chives

a generous squeeze of lemon juice

lots of freshly ground black pepper and a little salt

To make the dipping sauce, simply combine the ingredients in a small bowl.

To make the fish cakes, begin by mixing all the ingredients apart from the breadcrumbs in a large bowl and roughly mashing them together with a potato masher.

Using a tablespoon, divide the mixture into 16 golf-ball-sized lumps.

Place the breadcrumbs in a bowl. Take each fishy ball and press it down into the breadcrumbs to coat it.

Heat the oil or butter over medium heat and shallow fry the fish cakes (in batches if necessary) until golden brown, and serve with the dipping sauce.

Roast Salmon with Rosemary

Serves 2 • This is a very simple recipe, which should take about 15 minutes to make, but the end result looks very impressive. You will need a frying pan with an indestructible handle, as it is going in the oven.

If you choose to leave the skin on the salmon, which we recommend, remove the scales with a sharp knife and score the skin in a couple of places, otherwise the fish will curl up during cooking.

2 x 150g (5½oz) MSC-certified salmon fillets

2 good sprigs of rosemary, leaves removed from stalk and chopped

salt and freshly ground black pepper

olive oil

25g (1oz) butter

the juice of ½ lemon

50ml (2fl oz) white wine

Preheat the oven to 220ºC/425ºF/gas mark 7. Coat the salmon fillets with rosemary, salt and pepper. Fry them in a little olive oil over moderate heat for a minute or two on each side, starting with the skin side down. Then place the pan in the oven and roast for 10 minutes.

Take the pan out of the oven, wrapping a cloth around the handle to avoid burning your hand, then remove the fillets and keep them warm. Place the pan on a hob (without washing it), turn the heat to moderate and add the butter. As it melts, it will bubble and start to turn golden brown. When this happened, pour in the lemon juice and white wine. The pan will fizz up.

Immediately pour the sauce over the salmon fillets and serve with a light salad and sautéd potatoes.

W

I

N

T

E

R

Christmas is overwhelmingly the main feast in Britain, and feasts are inextricably linked with food. For many of the Duchy suppliers, the entire year has been geared towards the end of December. As the Christmas lights are switched on in the nation's high streets, the likes of Kelly's Turkeys in Essex and the Amiss family, who rear the Duchy Originals Wessex White geese in Devon, brace themselves for weeks of relentless activity. At Kelly's, for example, Christmas accounts for more than 95 per cent of annual turkey sales.

In this chapter, we focus on traditional festive centrepieces like goose and mincemeat, but we also look at some of the peripheral treats that are consumed in great quantity at this time of year. Christmas would not be the same without chocolates, for instance, or chipolatas/cocktail sausages to serve with the turkey or goose. The trail of these essential seasonal items leads back to dramatically contrasting locations: Brazil, the Dominican Republic and Guyana in the Western hemisphere and a factory in East Hull. We also examine the Duchy Originals cheeses in the Winter chapter, partly because we happened to visit the Stilton dairy in a blizzard, but largely because no Christmas spread is complete without a quality cheeseboard.

You will find recipes for all the Christmas classics here, from plum cake to turkey with the traditional trimmings, but we also provide some less obvious suggestions for feasting in grand style. There are few better things to do with leftover goose, for example, than make it into a cassoulet. Venison loin with port is a sumptuous dinner party dish, and the chapter closes with three decadent chocolate puddings.

STILTON

The village of Stilton in Cambridgeshire was the Watford Gap of the eighteenth century. Watford Gap, which is traditionally regarded as the dividing point between the North and South of England, is a motorway service station on the M1, one of the busiest roads in Europe. Stilton was a major staging post for coaches on the Great North Road, the most important highway of the day. A product with many of the qualities of the cheese that now bears the name of the village had been made in the East Midlands for at least a century, but it was popularised by the Bell Inn in Stilton, which sold it to travellers from all over the country.

Several places in the three counties in which genuine stilton is produced – Derbyshire, Nottinghamshire and Leicestershire – consider themselves the birthplace of the famous, blue-veined cheese, but Quenby Hall in Leicestershire has a stronger claim than most. According to legend, the housekeeper's daughter married the landlord of the Bell Inn and brought what is now called stilton with her. Certainly, it was at Quenby Hall that the production method for the cheese was first formalised. Now, Freddie de Lisle, the current owner of the magnificent Jacobean Hall, is reviving the manufacture of stilton in the place where it arguably began.

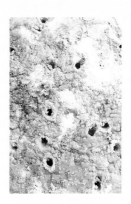

It is cold and misty on the day we visit Quenby Hall, and the surrounding area appears to be the one place in the country where snow is lying on the ground. Only when we approach the end of the long drive does the Hall loom impressively through

Top left and centre Sarah checks the consistency of the curd, which is then cut into cubes with a wire mesh.
Bottom left and centre John cuts the curds into large squares, which are then scooped up in buckets and transferred to the draining vat. **Main photograph** Stilton maturing. **Opposite** Quenby Hall.

the mist. By the time we park up, heavy snow is falling. We trudge to the front door, and are ushered into a splendid dining room, where Freddie awaits us with stilton and port.

Freddie is a quarter Peruvian, and he spends the first few minutes chatting enthusiastically about the merits of Peruvian food, particularly 'Pisco Sours' made with the national drink. Then we turn to the cheese. It is creamy, delicious and slightly 'mushroomy', with random veining rather than the uniform distribution of blue found in more mass-produced stilton. This kind of stilton is also drier than the Quenby product and with a thinner crust, but this is for reasons of

economy rather than taste, and Freddie is not prepared to cut corners. When we admit that we are unused to consuming stilton this early in the day, let alone drinking port, he seems almost surprised. The local farmers eat it all the time, he says, and his brother used to have it for breakfast from the age of six.

Before we move on to the dairy, Freddie gives us a tour of the house. Built in 1627, Quenby Hall has been little altered over the centuries. It is a period jewel, with intricate plaster ceilings, fireplaces and wood panelling. There are also numerous ancestral portraits and suits of armour.

Everything must be done gently, or the stilton
will lose its softness. 'Treat it like a baby'
is John's mantra.

En route to the new dairy, we stop off at the old one, which is now used as an atmospheric setting for functions and corporate events. The current dairy, by contrast, is thoroughly modern. Freddie introduces us to Sarah, the senior cheese-maker. Amazingly, until August 2005 she was a pet shop manager and had never made cheese in her life. She was trained up by John, a veteran cheese-maker whom Freddie pulled out of retirement. John has twenty years of stilton-making experience under his belt. One gets the impression that Sarah cannot believe her luck.

The first thing we see in the dairy is the 4,000 litre (7,000 pint) tank into which milk pasteurised on the premises is pumped and mixed with a couple of ounces of starter and mould cultures and some vegetarian rennet. It is then heated to 30.6ºC (87ºF) and left for two hours while the curds and whey separate. Freddie gives us glasses of whey to drink, and they are very refreshing. Once the curds have set to the consistency of blancmange - Sarah tests this by prodding them with her fingers - the whey is drained off. This takes about 40 minutes. The curds are then cut into small cubes with a wire mesh and lifted by bucket into a draining vat. When they have dried to the consistency of firm tofu, which takes 22 hours, they are crumbled by hand until they have a texture like scrambled eggs. Everything must

be done gently, or the stilton will lose its softness. 'Treat it like a baby' is John's mantra. Sarah refers to individual cheeses as 'she'.

The next phase of the cheese-making process begins with the transfer of the crumbled curds into hoop moulds with drain holes cut into their sides. A cup of salt is added to each mould, which is turned over several times over the ensuing days, initially every hour. The turning must be very rapid to avoid damage to the cheese, and as a result the procedure is known as 'breaking the neck'. After five days, the infant cheeses are robust enough to stand up unsupported, so the hoop moulds are removed. The cheeses are then rubbed with a knife to seal any cracks and holes. This prevents oxygen getting in, which would cause premature bluing.

At this point, the cheeses are placed on shelves in the adjacent maturing room. After six weeks, they are pierced with steel spikes to let oxygen in, which precipitates the desired bluing. The cheeses are pierced again one week later, then they are left until they have formed slightly sticky orange coats, the signal that they have matured. They are typically twelve weeks old at this stage, but Freddie maintains that stilton is at its best at 22 weeks. We make a mental note to follow this advice and refrain from eating the booty with which we leave for two and a half months.

Cheeseboard

The selection of after-dinner cheeses is all too often an afterthought. Instead, they should be regarded as comprising a fully fledged course. A good cheeseboard is visually stunning, with contrasting flavours, appearances and textures. It should include some varieties that people recognise and are comfortable with, but also at least one cheese that is special, rare or unusual. Johnny, for instance, is a big fan of Yarg, a crumbly white cheese from Cornwall that comes wrapped in nettle leaves.

Duchy Originals already sells an excellent Cornish brie and the stilton described on the previous pages. Two varieties of organic cheddar, one smoked and one 'regular' are also in the pipeline, plus an ale-washed rind cheese similar to brie and territorial cheeses - a Wensleydale, Double Gloucester and Red Leicester. The Duchy cheeses have the necessary contrasting characteristics to furnish a superior cheeseboard by themselves. They are all, naturally, of top quality, but below we give some tips for what to look for in general terms when buying these big-hitting varieties.

Stilton Visually, desirable characteristics include a reasonably thick layer of mould on the outside and a good veining structure within. Chalkiness in the cheese, as opposed to glossiness, is a sign that it is immature and should be avoided. Look for an open texture (i.e. not too compacted), which indicates that the stilton has not been pressurised. The flavour should be smooth, buttery, rich and full bodied. The cheese should melt in the mouth and have a pungent after-note.

Brie Look for a clean white bloom on the outside; avoid specimens with brown patches. The inside of the cheese should be ripe and runny. Good brie has a smooth mushroomy flavour and a somewhat straw-like taste.

Cheddar A darkish rind with a slight mould growth is a positive sign. The skin should be smooth and not blotchy. Inside, look for an open texture, and don't be put off by cracks running through the cheese. The colour of the centre can be slightly lighter than the outer area.

Fine cheddar has great depth of flavour, and the taste should improve as you chew it. The cheese shouldn't have a kick to it; rather, you are looking for a smooth, caramelised taste with a slight sweetness.

Beetroot Soup with Organic Vintage Cheddar Cheese Bread Croûtons

Serves 4+ • This soup is a festive deep red, and the beetroot is highly seasonal. It is best made with beef stock, but will still be extremely tasty if you choose to make a vegetarian version.

THE SOUP

2 medium carrots, sliced

2 garlic cloves, chopped

150g (5½oz) fresh tomatoes, chopped

1 large onion, sliced

50g (2oz) unsalted butter

1 tablespoon balsamic vinegar

1 teaspoon sugar

1 litre (1¾ pints) beef stock (or water mixed with 2 teaspoons organic vegetable bouillon)

300g (10½oz) potatoes (not new ones), peeled and diced

1 teaspoon chopped thyme

500g (18oz) cooked beetroot, peeled (boil with the skin on for 30 minutes, then rub off the skin and trim each end)

salt and ground black pepper

150ml (¼ pint) sour cream

THE CROÛTONS

3-4 slices of Duchy Originals vintage cheddar bread, cut into small cubes

salt and pepper

2 teaspoons chopped thyme

1 tablespoon olive oil

To make the croûtons, first toss the bread cubes around in a bowl along with a little salt and pepper, the thyme and olive oil.
Dry fry the bread cubes over low heat, stirring regularly until they are nice and brown, and reserve until needed.
To make the soup, begin by frying the carrots, garlic, tomatoes and onion in the butter over low to moderate heat until softened. Keep the lid on the saucepan, except to give the mixture an occasional stir.
Add the balsamic vinegar and the sugar and continue to cook for a minute or two.
Pour in the beef stock and add the potatoes and thyme. Simmer for 15-20 minutes until the potatoes are soft. Then add the beetroot and simmer for a further 5 minutes.
Blend the soup until smooth and season with the salt and pepper.
Swirl in the sour cream and serve immediately, garnished with the croûtons.

Celery and Duchy Originals Stilton Soup

Serves 4+ • Stilton is great in soups, but it needs to be accompanied by strong-tasting vegetables or their flavour will be overwhelmed. Celery fits the bill admirably and provides a slightly sharp edge that complements the creaminess of the soup.

½ medium onion (100g/3½oz)

½ medium leek (around 60g/2½oz)

350g (12oz) sliced celery

30g (1oz) unsalted butter

1 litre (1¾ pints) chicken stock, or water mixed with 2 teaspoons (10g/½oz) vegetable bouillon

300g (10½oz) peeled, diced potatoes. Use a mashing variety.

150g (5½oz) Duchy Originals stilton, crumbled, including the rind if desired

6 fresh sage leaves

Gently fry the onion, leek and celery in the butter with the lid on the saucepan, stirring occasionally, for 10 minutes or until the vegetables are soft.
Add the chicken stock, or water and vegetable bouillon, then the potatoes. Simmer for 20 minutes until the potato is cooked.
Add the stilton and sage leaves, and blend the soup until smooth.
Serve with a herb salad.

Quenby Hall Blues (Stilton Biscuits)

Makes about 25 biscuits • This recipe was devised by Michelle Padwick, the wife of Freddie de Lisle's tenant farmer at Quenby Hall. We ate some of these biscuits when we went to Leicestershire and they were excellent.

75g (3oz) Duchy Originals stilton

1 teaspoon English mustard

150g (5½oz) plain flour

100g (3½oz) butter, at room temperature

½ teaspoon Maldon sea salt

½ teaspoon cracked black pepper

75g (3oz) chopped walnuts

Place all the ingredients, apart from the walnuts, in food processor and pulse until they start to form a ball. At this point, add the walnuts and pulse for a few more seconds.
Turn the dough out onto a floured surface and divide it into two pieces. Roll each half into an even 'sausage' about 12cm (4½in) long and 4-5cm (1½-2in) in diameter. Place in the fridge and leave to chill for 30 minutes.
Preheat the oven to 180ºC/350ºF/gas mark 4. In the meantime, slice the dough sausages into discs about 1cm (½in) thick and lay them on a greased baking tray or silicone sheet. Bake the biscuits for 18-20 minutes, then leave them to cool on a wire rack. They will keep in an airtight container for up to a fortnight.

Vintage Cheddar Crostini with Stilton Pesto

Smeared with a tangy, herby and very more-ish pesto, these crostini are ideal for cocktail parties and soirées in general. If you don't have any vintage cheddar cheese bread, any decent loaf will produce results almost as good.

50g (2oz) walnut pieces, dry baked in the oven for 5 minutes at 180°C/350°F/ gas mark 4

10 sage leaves

2 teaspoons chopped fresh thyme

a good pinch of Maldon organic sea salt

a grind of black pepper

4 tablespoons olive oil

juice of ½ lemon

50g (2oz) Duchy Originals stilton, crumbled

Duchy Originals vintage cheddar cheese bread, cut into small squares and toasted

Roughly blend the walnut pieces, sage, thyme, sea salt, pepper, olive oil and lemon juice.

Turn the mixture out into a bowl and mash in the stilton with a fork. This is meant to be a rough pesto, so don't worry if little lumps of walnut and stilton remain.

Spread the pesto on to the toasted squares of vintage cheddar cheese bread and pass around immediately.

Stilton and Mushroom Muffins

Serves 1 • Often, the success of a dish lies in its simplicity. This is one of the easiest recipes in the book, but the results are sophisticated and highly satisfying.

We've shown you how to make English Muffins on page 69. For a delicious snack or light tea, all you now need is some creamy stilton, a few large, flat field mushrooms and some sage leaves.

Each muffin makes two toasted Stilton and Mushroom Muffins, and we recommend two per person.

1 muffin

butter

2 field mushrooms, roughly the same diameter as the muffin

2 thick slices of Duchy Originals stilton

4 fresh sage leaves

salt and freshly ground black pepper

Preheat the oven to 220°C/425°F/gas mark 7.

Split the muffin down the middle and spread each half with butter. Place the mushrooms on top and cover with the stilton and sage leaves.

Season with a little salt and a generous quantity of pepper, bake for 10 minutes and serve immediately.

Cheddar and Roasted Pepper Tart

Serves 4 • This is a fine tart for impromptu entertaining, or at least reasonably impromptu, as it only takes about half an hour to make, if you roast the pepper in advance.

Use a shallow, non-stick pizza pan approximately 1cm ('/₂in) deep with a 1cm ('/₂in) lip.

THE PASTRY

see the Cheese Pastry recipe on page 204

THE FILLING

1 large red pepper

150g (5½oz) mature cheddar, roughly grated

120g (4½oz) crème fraîche

1 large egg with 1 extra yolk

2 teaspoons chopped fresh thyme

½ teaspoon smoked ground paprika or regular ground paprika

salt and freshly ground black pepper

First, preheat the oven to 240ºC/475ºF/gas mark 9 and bake the red pepper for 15 minutes until nice and charred, then leave to cool. Peel off the skin, remove the seeds and slice into thin strips. Set aside.

To make the pastry, follow the recipe on page 204.

Lower the oven to 200ºC/400ºF/gas mark 6.

Roll out the pastry to the approximate size of the pizza pan and lay it over it. Press the pastry down into the pan, but to get that home-made look, don't trim round the sides.

Now make the filling. Mix the cheddar with the crème fraîche, egg, thyme, salt and pepper, and spread the mixture onto the pastry, right to the sides.

Lay the roasted pepper strips in a random, higgledy-piggledy manner, and powder the surface with paprika.

Bake in the oven for 15–20 minutes until the cheese is browned. Eat while still warm.

Warm Salad of Brie with Roasted Tomatoes and Duchy Originals Olive Oil and Fresh Herb Dressing

Serves 4 • Brie and tomato accompany each other perfectly, particularly in the presence of crunchy French bread and herby salad dressing.

This warm salad, with its globules of melted brie, makes an excellent Winter starter.

6 tomatoes

olive oil

salt and freshly ground black pepper

a mixture of salad leaves, e.g. rocket, romaine, chard, frizée, cos, oak leaf, baby leaf spinach

Duchy Originals olive oil and fresh herb dressing

16 black olives

1 medium red onion, sliced into rings

basil leaves

8 chunky slices of Duchy Originals brie, slightly smaller than the bread as they will become runny as they melt

8 slices of French bread, toasted

Cut the tomatoes in half, season with olive oil, salt and pepper, and roast in a low oven (130ºC/275ºF/gas mark 1) for 1½ hours.
Toss the salad leaves with the dressing and place in 4 separate bowls. Scatter with the olives, red onion, tomatoes and basil leaves.
Place the brie on the slices of French bread and give them a quick blast under a hot grill.
Lay the toasts onto the salads and serve immediately.
An equally delicious version can be made with goat's cheese instead of brie.

Chicken Breast Salad with Honeyed Carrots and Wensleydale

Serves 2–3 • This is a good Winter salad because it is meant to be eaten warm. There's nothing worse than cold lettuce against your teeth on a freezing day.

The Wensleydale gives this salad a slight but welcome bite. Arrange the salad on a large shallow serving dish.

4 medium carrots, peeled and sliced thinly lengthways

20g (¾oz) Duchy Selections honey

30g (1oz) unsalted butter

1 teaspoon chopped fresh thyme

salt and freshly ground black pepper

2 medium organic chicken breast fillets, skin on or off according to preference

the leaves from a small stem of rosemary

juice of ½ lemon

a small bowlful of baby spinach leaves

100g (3½oz) Wensleydale cheese, crumbled

a handful of shelled pumpkin seeds, dry roasted for about 5 minutes at 180ºC/350ºF/gas mark 4

a small sprig of flat leaf parsley, leaves removed from stalk

Duchy Originals honey mustard vinaigrette

Gently fry the carrot for 20 minutes with the honey, butter and thyme, and season to taste.
Season the chicken breasts with the rosemary leaves, salt, pepper and lemon juice and fry over medium heat for 5-6 minutes on each side.
Arrange the spinach leaves on the serving dish.
Roughly slice the chicken, then add it to the salad along with the carrot.
Sprinkle with the Wensleydale, pumpkin seeds and flat leaf parsley, and serve with Duchy Originals honey mustard vinaigrette.

SAUSAGES

The Duchy Originals and Duchy Selections range of sausages is made by Cranswick PLC in Helsinki Road, East Hull. The factory is known as Mr Lazenby's after a Teesside-based firm of speciality sausage makers purchased by the company in 1998.

'Normal' premium sausages have a pork content of 65 per cent, but Duchy ones are 78-85 per cent meat, making them 'super premium' by anyone's standards. In sharp contrast with lesser brands, whose casings are frequently made from reconstituted collagen, they are enclosed by natural membranes.

The organic Honey & Rosemary Chipolatas and Cocktail Sausages are made with meat from animals including the delightful pigs we met in the Spring chapter. The other sausages in the range, which are sold under the Duchy Selections label, contain high quality free range pork. There are two main reasons for this. First, Duchy Originals has long supported British free range farmers as well as their organic colleagues. Second, there is currently simply not enough organic pork of a suitable standard available to meet demand. The free range pigs in question are reared in considerable comfort in Yorkshire and East Anglia as well as other farms in the UK, where they live outdoors in family groups and have plenty of mud baths to wallow in. Their farmers observe the highest animal welfare standards, and common practices like tail docking and tooth clipping are strictly prohibited.

Duchy Originals Big Breakfast

The constituents of the pictured breakfast, which would certainly tempt us out of our beds on a cold Winter morning, are Duchy streaky bacon and pork and herb sausages, with mushrooms, tomatoes, potato hash and a glass of tomato juice on the side. We don't want to insult your intelligence by telling you how to cook the majority of these basic items, but we do provide the recipe for the potato hash below, as its preparation is less obvious. We also have a tip for you. It is easier, and healthier, to grill rather than fry the other components of your breakfast, which you will appreciate if you've burned the midnight oil the night before. Simply place all the ingredients, including the mushrooms and tomatoes, under a hot grill, and remove them successively as they become cooked.

Potato Hash

Serves 2 • Potato hash has an interesting texture, which is soft and crunchy at the same time. It is also very good with baked beans.

1 medium potato

cooking oil

Grate the potato quite thickly, then take a handful of the gratings and squeeze out the juices with your fist. Repeat until all the potato has been used up. This will leave you with compacted patties, which you should fry in oil heated to 180ºC (350ºF) until golden brown.

Hotpot with Chipolatas

Makes a large pot-full • Bizarrely, in the eighteenth century a hotpot was a kind of punch. This, however, is a wholesome Winter stew, so thick you can stand a spoon in it. Like many stews, it will taste even better when it's a day old and the flavours have had time to meld.

340g (12oz) Duchy Selections pork chipolatas

½ leek, washed and roughly sliced

1 medium onion, roughly diced

2 garlic cloves, chopped

1 heaped teaspoon paprika

150g (5½oz) red pepper, roughly chopped

1 tablespoon olive oil

50g (2oz) tomato purée

a glass of red wine

2 teaspoons chopped fresh thyme

2 bay leaves

a pinch (and no more) of dried sage

1 litre (1¾ pints) chicken stock

1 medium potato, diced

300g (10½oz) chopped tomatoes

1 tablespoon Worcestershire sauce

150g (5½oz) cooked white beans (any variety you like)

salt and freshly ground pepper

a handful of flat leaf parsley, chopped

Briefly fry the chipolata sausages over moderate heat, then leave in the pan until cool. Roughly slice and reserve, remembering to save all the juices for the hotpot.

In a large saucepan, fry the leek, onion, garlic, paprika and red pepper in the olive oil over medium heat for around 10 minutes, stirring frequently. Add the tomato purée and red wine and cook on gently for another 5 minutes.

Add the thyme, bay leaves, sage, chicken stock, potato, tomatoes, Worcestershire sauce and sliced chipolatas. Simmer for 1 hour. Don't worry if the liquid reduces quite a bit; we have allowed for this in the recipe.

Finally, add the beans, seasoning and flat leaf parsley.

This hotpot freezes beautifully and will store in the fridge for at least 3 days.

GEESE

On the day chosen for our visit to the Devon farm where the Duchy Originals geese are reared, we make an elementary mistake. We drive past Higher Fingle Farm several times because we are trying to locate it with our eyes rather than our ears. The moment we wind down the windows, we are led to our destination by a chorus of honking.

Neville and Rhona Amiss have been rearing organic Wessex White geese ever since their bed and breakfast business in Exmoor collapsed during the foot and mouth crisis of 2001. On 1st December 2004, they awoke to find that half their geese, about 250 birds, had disappeared, having fallen victim to well-organised rustlers. This prompted them to move to Higher Fingle Farm, a sixty-acre holding in hilly country outside Exeter. They arrived on Lady Day (25th March) the following year, and although there was no mains electricity at first and they needed to allow a year to convert the farm to the organic system, they are delighted with their new base. The geese seem to grow faster at the higher elevation and their feed is easier to keep dry. Exmoor, by contrast, is one of the wettest places in the country.

Before we meet the geese, we have a cup of tea in the Amiss's delightful farmhouse, and meet their five children: Elsa (7), Alfred (4), Dora (2) and twins Harold and Percy (11 months). Like their mother, they all have flaming red hair. Rhona is a country girl, originally from Standlake in Oxfordshire, but Neville grew up in Sunderland and scarcely even saw a farm before his late teens.

As Neville explains, the Amisses don't actually breed geese. The organic goslings arrive in April or May, within a week of being hatched by John Byrnes in South

Moulton. Young geese are not waterproof and are very vulnerable to hypothermia, so for the first ten weeks of their lives they are kept indoors under gas brooders. They are only allowed outside once they are fully feathered. The goslings are fed on 'chick crumb' for their first two or three weeks, then grower pellets. At ten weeks they graduate to grass, and from August they have a wheat-based diet. This regime is responsible for the adult birds' lovely firm, yellow fat. Artificial feed, as Neville tells us, tends to produce soft fat, which results in less tasty meat. Soft fat is also less satisfactory as a cooking medium, and a supply of high quality fat is potentially one of the great perks of roasting a goose, particularly if you use it to baste roast potatoes.

When we have downed our tea, we amble down to the large, open-sided barn where the majority of the farm's 200 geese are in residence. Neville hopes to increase the population to 500 in due course. They are usually out in the fields from 8am to dusk, but today they have been kept in until our arrival to facilitate photography. The first thing that strikes us is the geese's herd-like behaviour. They tend to wander in unison round an enormous pillar of straw in the centre of the barn. One minute they are all honking, the next a sudden silence breaks out.

While Neville and Jonathan the photographer position themselves downhill at the mouth of the field, Elsa, the oldest daughter, is charged with releasing the geese from the barn. When she opens the gate, there is a bedlam of rushing birds. When the resulting pile disassembles itself, we are dismayed to see one of the geese at the bottom lying motionless. Johnny rather nervously walks down to the field and tells Neville he thinks one of his geese may be dead. Neville strides up to the barn,

picks up the afflicted bird and unkinks its neck. It is miraculously restored to life and happily waddles along to join its comrades.

Chaperoned by the other Amiss children, the flock marches down to the field where Jonathan is waiting by the gate to get some 'head-on' shots. When the birds get to him, there is another brief pile-up and he disappears in a storm of feathers. Geese are nervous birds at the best of times, perhaps understandably in a world of foxes and rustlers, and their jumpiness is not aided by the sparrow hawk buzzing overhead. In next to no time, however, they are grazing contentedly all around the extensive field.

To end our tour, Neville shows us around the state-of-the-art abattoir which is currently under construction. The killing of the Christmas geese begins on 2nd December. Many farmers keep them indoors for the last month, but the Amisses do not follow suit. As Neville explains, geese are creatures of habit and inclined to go a little stir-crazy when confined for long periods. He also wants them to have a trouble-free waddle to the abattoir when the time comes, and this is unlikely if it is their first excursion for several weeks.

The abattoir is divided into four sections. The first is the killing and plucking room. Plucking is a two-part process. The larger feathers are removed by machine. The birds are then dipped in paraffin wax, which is peeled off by hand, taking the down with it. The geese then progress to the hanging room, where they spend two weeks at a temperature of 5ºC (41ºF) or slightly below while the flesh matures. They are then eviscerated in the dressing room, with the giblets staying with their own bird. Finally, they are moved to the cold storage room to await dispatch.

Below Rhona and Neville Amiss with their Wessex White geese. The geese are kept in the barn until they are ten weeks old, when their feathers are fully grown and able to protect them from the weather.

Roasted Goose with Duchy Streaky Bacon, Sausage Meat and Chestnuts

Serves 6 • Geese have been eaten at important feasts since time immemorial, probably because our ancestors noted that wild geese arrived and departed at agriculturally important times of year and invested their migratory patterns with great significance.

For this recipe you will need a goose weighing 4.5-5.5kg (10-12lb) including the giblets. Trim any excess fat from the bird, but don't throw it away; use it as a roasting medium for potatoes.

THE GRAVY

the giblets from the goose

1 medium carrot

1 stick of celery

1 medium onion, sliced in half

2 garlic cloves

1 bay leaf

a sprig of thyme

glass of red wine, if you like

THE STUFFING

500g (18oz) fresh minced organic pork

250g (9oz) cooked and peeled sweet chestnuts, chopped. Fresh ones should be grilled for 10 minutes before peeling or use ready prepared cooked whole chestnuts

1 level tablespoon chopped fresh sage

150g (5½oz) roughly chopped onion, softened in butter

100g (3½oz) fresh breadcrumbs made from Duchy Originals mixed seed or any other fresh bread. Pulse in the food processor until crumbed

1 goose liver, diced

50g (2oz) unsalted butter

½ teaspoon ground mace

½ teaspoon fine or flaky salt

lots of freshly ground black pepper

a generous grating of nutmeg

1 heaped tablespoon chopped parsley

1 heaped teaspoon chopped thyme

100g (3½oz) chopped Duchy Originals organic streaky bacon plus 4 whole rashers

To make the gravy, you first need to make a giblet stock. Roast the giblets and the carrot, celery, onion and garlic for 20 minutes at 200ºC/400ºF/gas mark 6. Place the cooked ingredients in a pan along with the bay leaf and thyme and just cover with water. Then simply simmer until the goose is ready. Don't worry if the liquid reduces by half - the more it evaporates the better the flavour.

To stuff and cook the goose, first preheat the oven to 240ºC/475ºF/gas mark 9.

Mix all the ingredients for the stuffing apart from the 4 rashers of bacon together in a large bowl, using either your fingers or a spoon according to your inclination.

Stuff the goose with the filling, lightly pushing it into the cavity. Plug the open end with the 4 slices of streaky bacon.

Take a skewer and pass it through the tops of the thighs, via the open vent. Then make a loop in a short length of string and lasso it over one end of the skewer. Pass the string over the bird and loop it over the other end of the skewer. Pull the lasso in so that the vent is half closed and the legs are drawn in tight to the body. Then take another skewer and length of string and repeat the process with the wings.

Now season the goose, rubbing it with salt and pepper and a little excess goose fat from the cavity.

Roast 20 minutes, then turn the heat down to 180ºC/350ºF/gas mark 4 and cook for a further 2¼ hours until the goose and stuffing are cooked through and clear juices run when pierced by a skewer.

Remove the goose from the oven, place it on a chopping board and let it rest for at least 20 minutes before you touch it.

While the goose is resting, make the gravy. To do this, ladle off the excess fat from the giblet stock, strain the stock into the tin in which you roasted the goose (discarding the giblets and vegetables) and heat it up on the stove. Use a large spoon to scrape all the caramelised bits that have adhered to the tin into the gravy. You may also want to add a glass of red wine. Finally, season the gravy with salt and pepper and pour it into a gravy boat.

Serve the goose with red cabbage and roast potatoes, accompanied by apple or gooseberry sauce.

Goose: Stock, Confit, Rillettes and Paté

Let us assume you have equipped yourself with a medium-sized organic goose weighing about 4.5kg (10lb). You have two main options. The first, of course, is to roast it, and we give detailed instructions on page 179. The alternative is to dismantle the bird and convert it into several delicacies. One goose will furnish you with a superior stock, a melting confit, a snack of crispy wings, plus rillettes and paté. You will need to allocate half a day to achieve this yield, but it will be well worth it.

First, you need to deal with the goose as a whole. Begin by removing and reserving the liver. Then take the legs off for the confit. To do this, place the goose breast side up and cut into the skin where the legs divide from the breast. Bend the legs back and carefully cut them away from the rest of the bird. Cut as close to the carcass as possible, and make sure you include the scalloped area of flesh near the backbone.

Now remove the wishbone, to make the breast meat easier to remove, and fillet off the breasts and remove the wings. Don't worry if you don't do this prettily, because you are going to cook the breasts down into rillettes.

Finally, remove all the fat and skin (apart from the skin on the legs) and reserve.

YOU WILL NOW HAVE:

a pile of skin and fat (about 1.5kg/3lb 5oz)

bones and giblets

2 wings

breast meat for the rillettes (600g/1¼lb)

the liver (200g/7oz)

2 whole legs

GOOSE STOCK

It would be foolish not to make goose stock from the bones and giblets, and it is an essential ingredient in various recipes in this book, such as the cassoulet on page 182. Roast the bones and giblets for 40 minutes in a hot oven (220ºC/425ºF/gas mark 7) along with a carrot, 2 chopped sticks of celery and an onion. Pour off and reserve the fat, then transfer the bones and giblets to a large pot and just cover them with water. (You may want to break up the carcass to get a better fit). Simmer for 2 to 3 hours, skimming occasionally, and the stock is ready.

THE WINGS

To make an excellent snack to sustain you while you deal with the rest of the goose, season the wings with a little salt, pepper and paprika, and bake them for 25 minutes at 220ºC/425ºF/gas mark 7 until the skin is crispy.

THE FAT

Goose fat is an integral part of the following recipes, and you need to process it before you use it. It can also be used to make the best roast potatoes you have ever eaten. Your initial 1.5kg (3lb 5oz) will yield about 1.1kg (2½lb) of pure clear fat.

Mince all the skin and fat from the goose or chop them into small pieces. Place in a saucepan with the fat left over from the stock, and bring to a simmer. After about 5 minutes, the fat will run clear. Strain it, and discard all the particles left over.

Goose Leg Confit

Serves 4 • For this delicacy, you need a tight-fitting casserole dish and an airtight container for storage. Serve with mushrooms sautéd in garlic and parsley, or cold, accompanied by a green salad.

2 legs from a 4.5kg (10lb) goose

a teaspoon flaky sea salt

4 cloves

a couple of sprigs of thyme, chopped

2 garlic cloves, cut into 8 pieces

freshly ground black pepper

grated nutmeg

400g (14oz) goose fat (see opposite)

2 bay leaves

Lay the goose legs on a plate, skin side down. Rub them with the salt, then press together via their dark fleshy sides. Place in an airtight container and store in the fridge overnight. Preheat the oven to 180ºC/350ºF/gas mark 4. Lay the goose legs in an oven dish, skin side up. Cover them with the cloves, thyme, garlic, some pepper and a little grated nutmeg. Rub the mixture in, and leave the legs to rest for 15 minutes. Then add the goose fat and bay leaves, cover the dish, and bake for 2½ hours. Transfer to an airtight container and store in the fridge. Sealed, they will keep for several months.
To eat, scrape off the fat, then bake in a hot oven (220ºC/425ºF/gas mark 7) for about 25 minutes until the skin is crispy.

Goose Rillettes

Rillettes are essentially an up-market form of potted meat. They are perfect for picnics, but don't leave them in the sun for too long or they will melt. Serve with crusty bread. The rillettes will keep for about 2 weeks, but once you break the seals, eat them within 5 days.

600g (1¼lb) goose breast meat, roughly cubed

400g (14oz) goose fat

2 bay leaves

2 sprigs of thyme

2 cloves

salt and pepper

Place all ingredients in a saucepan with 250ml (9fl oz) water. Simmer very slowly for 2 hours, stirring occasionally. Make sure the meat doesn't start to brown. If it does, add a little more water.
Strain off the fat and leave the meat to cool. Then, using either your fingers or a pair of forks, tease the goose flesh into strands.
Place the meat back in the fat and briefly bring to boiling point.
Pack the meat into small ceramic pots along with enough fat to just cover, reserving about 100ml (3½fl oz) of the fat for later.
Cover the pots and leave the rillettes to set in the fridge.
Re-melt the remaining fat and pour it over the pots to form seals.

Goose Liver Paté

Goose liver paté is notoriously delicious, and this version has the advantage of not depending on organs made unnaturally large by the force-feeding of the poor birds.

50ml (2fl oz) clarified butter (see method)

1 goose liver, weighing about 200g (7oz)

50g (2oz) unsalted butter

a large garlic clove, finely chopped

a sprig of thyme, chopped

a good splash of brandy (30ml/1fl oz)

50ml (2fl oz) crème fraîche

½ teaspoon mustard powder

Maldon sea salt and pepper

grated nutmeg

To make the clarified butter, gently heat up rather more than 50g (2oz) of regular butter in a small pan until the fat has separated from the whey. Ladle off and reserve the top layer – the clarified butter – and discard the whey.
Trim the liver and gently fry in half the butter with the garlic and thyme until cooked. Add the brandy and the rest of the butter and cook for a few minutes.
Pour into a blender and add the crème fraîche, mustard powder, and a little pepper and grated nutmeg. Blend until smooth. (If you want a smoother texture, pass the paté through a fine sieve).
Mix in a little salt, then spoon it into 2 small ceramic pots. Press the paté down, then pour over the clarified butter to seal and leave to set in the fridge.

Cassoulet Made with Leftover Duck or Goose

Serves 4 • Everyone loves a rich stew, full of meat and root vegetables. This one is useful as well as deeply satisfying: in the tradition of many great stews, much of the flavour comes from leftovers. Cassoulet originates from the South West of France, where duck and geese are staples.

the carcass from your goose or duck

340g (12oz) Duchy pork chipolatas

2 medium carrots, peeled and roughly chopped

2 sticks of celery, roughly chopped

1 medium onion, roughly chopped

1 tablespoon goose or duck fat

1 tablespoon plain flour

1 heaped tablespoon tomato purée

leftover goose or duck meat. A breast or a leg will be enough, but if you have more, use it

4 sprigs of thyme

3 bay leaves

400g (14oz) cooked haricot beans

salt and freshly ground black pepper

2 tablespoons fresh bread crumbs, mixed with a teaspoon of fat and a pinch or two of salt

First, make the stock. Break the goose or duck carcass down, cram it into a pan and just cover with water. Simmer for an hour or two with any leftover gravy, which will intensify the flavour.

Lightly fry the chipolatas, allow them to cool and roughly slice them. Pour the juices into the stock.

Fry the carrot, celery and onion in the goose fat over medium heat for about 10 minutes, until soft.

Turn the heat right down and add the flour and tomato purée. Stir in thoroughly, then slowly start adding the hot stock, stirring vigorously as you do so.

Once all the stock is in (you should have at least 1 litre (1¾ pints); if there isn't enough, top up with water), add the chipolatas, leftover meat, thyme and bay leaves. Simmer for 20 minutes, stirring frequently, then add the beans and season with salt and pepper.

The best way to serve this stew is in individual earthenware bowls or a large ceramic dish.

Fill the pots or dish with the cassoulet and sprinkle with the breadcrumbs. Grill for a couple of minutes until the breadcrumbs are golden brown. Serve immediately with hunks of bread.

Turkey Breast Joint with Sloe Gin Cranberry Sauce

Serves 4 • You don't have to slave over a hot stove all day in order to cook your main Christmas meal. Here we show you how to make a classic dinner for 4 people in about 2 hours, plus a tiny bit of prep work the day before if you make the sauce in advance. The Duchy Originals Cranberry Sauce is excellent as it is, but when you boil it up with sloe gin it enters another realm entirely. The sauce will be a real talking point, and if stored in an airtight container, will keep for 2 weeks in the fridge.

1 jar Duchy Originals cranberry sauce

100ml (3½fl oz) sloe gin

1 Duchy Originals turkey breast joint (weighing 1.2kg/2lb 12oz)

salt and freshly ground black pepper

dried sage

olive oil

roasting potatoes and parsnips, peeled, boiled for 10 minutes, drained, then covered in olive oil, salt, pepper and chopped fresh thyme

340g (12oz) Duchy chipolatas, pork or honey and rosemary according to your preference

1 pot Duchy Originals poultry gravy

vegetables of your choice, e.g. Brussels sprouts

Combine the cranberry sauce and sloe gin in a saucepan, and boil for 5 minutes until thick and syrupy. Pour the sauce into a sealed container, allow it to cool, and store in the fridge until needed.

Preheat the oven to 200ºC/400ºF/gas mark 6. Season the turkey with salt, pepper, dried sage and olive oil and bake for slightly over an hour. Place the potatoes and parsnips in the oven at the same time.

10 minutes before the turkey is ready, fry up the chipolatas and heat up the water for the other vegetables.

Take the turkey out of the oven and inspect the potatoes and parsnips. If they need a little more time, place them on the top shelf while the turkey rests for 10 minutes or so. In the meantime, cook the vegetables and heat up the gravy.

Suddenly everything is ready and there was very little stress.

Carve the turkey and serve with the sloe gin cranberry sauce.

Roast KellyBronze Turkey with Trimmings

The KellyBronze turkeys sold by Duchy Originals and featured in the Spring chapter require a shorter cooking time than the 20 minutes per pound traditionally regarded as the norm. There are three reasons for this. First, it has become fashionable to cook the stuffing separately from the bird or in the neck cavity only as suggested below. This allows hot air to circulate in the main cavity, which reduces the cooking time and consequently produces more succulent meat. Second, as Paul Kelly suggests, the 'old' formula probably reflected the then common practice of buying the Christmas turkey frozen. Finally, the KellyBronze is mature when it is sold, and consequently has a better marbling of fat than the average turkey. Fat heats more quickly than protein, so the bird cooks more quickly.

Nobody knows the KellyBronze better than Paul's mother Mollie, so we have followed her advice regarding cooking times and method.

ROASTING TIMES BY OVEN READY-WEIGHT AT 180°C/350°F/GAS MARK 4

4kg (8.8 lb)	2 hours
5kg (11 lb)	2 hours 15 minutes
6Kg (13.2 lb)	2 hours 30 minutes
7kg (15.4 lb)	2 hours 45 minutes
8Kg (17.6 lb)	2 hours 55 minutes
9kg (19.8 lb)	3 hours 10 minutes
10kg (22 lb)	3 hours 25 minutes
11kg (24.3 lb)	3 hours 40 minutes

PREPARATION AND COOKING

Remove the bird from the fridge and wash it, then let it sit at room temperature for 2 hours before cooking. Before you put the turkey in the oven, sprinkle it with salt and pepper and insert a large peeled onion in the body cavity for extra flavour. Place the bird in a roasting tin with its breast down. This will allow the fat deposits in its back to percolate the breast meat during cooking.

Roast the turkey at 180°C/350°F/gas mark 4 for the time indicated in the table, adjusting the temperature if you know your oven dial tends to over- or under-estimate it. We recommend that you refrain from covering the bird with tin foil, as this tends to steam the meat rather than roast it. You will also get crispier skin in the absence of a foil barrier.

Thirty minutes before the end of its cooking time, turn the turkey over (beware of hot fat) to brown the breast. The bird is cooked when the juices run clear when you pierce the inside of the thigh with a skewer. If they run pink, return the turkey to the oven and repeat the skewer test every 15 minutes until the desired result is achieved. Leave the bird to rest for 30 minutes before carving. **Serve** with Duchy Originals cranberry sauce.

The Trimmings

GRAVY

The simplest way to make the gravy to accompany your turkey is as follows: first remove the bird from the baking tray and pour in a splash of hot water and a glass of red wine. Swirl the contents of the tray around, and bring to the boil over moderate heat while scraping any caramelised bits of turkey into the gravy with a wooden spoon. Skim off the fat with a ladle and pour the gravy into a suitable serving receptacle. It will be very liquid, which is just how we like it. If you prefer a thicker gravy, sift some flour or cornflour into the tray at the swirling/scraping stage and make sure you stir it in well to avoid the formation of lumps.

SAUSAGES WRAPPED IN BACON

The Duchy Originals honey and rosemary cocktail sausages were specifically designed with this essential Christmas accoutrement in mind. Wrap the sausages in Duchy streaky bacon, place them on a baking tray and cook till golden at 190°C/375°F/gas mark 5. This should take about 30 minutes.

POTATOES AND PARSNIPS

Peel the potatoes and cut them and the parsnips into appropriately sized chunks. Par-boil the vegetables for 10 minutes, then drain them through the gap between your pan and its lid and give the pan a good shake. This will give the potatoes and parsnips nice fluffy surfaces. Place them on a non-stick tray, baste generously with olive oil or goose fat and sprinkle with sea salt. If you like garlic, add a few big cloves or even an entire head. You might also want to throw in some sprigs of rosemary and/or thyme. They will emerge thoroughly crispy.

Place the tray of vegetables in the oven in which your turkey is roasting at 180°C/350°F/gas mark 4 about 40 minutes before the end of its cooking time. When you remove the bird, turn the potatoes and parsnips over, give them a good basting and increase the heat to 200-220°C/400-425°F/gas mark 6-7. Leave the vegetables to continue roasting for 30 minutes while the turkey rests.

The above method works equally well for other root vegetables - carrots, parsnips, swede, celeriac, jerusalem artichokes, you name it.

Spinach and Pine Kernel Stuffing

This recipe comes via Mollie Kelly, courtesy of British Turkey. It produces a light, savoury stuffing with none of the stodginess of some versions.

1 tablespoon vegetable oil

1 medium onion, peeled and chopped

2-4 garlic cloves, peeled and crushed

1 carrot, about 100g (3½oz) peeled and grated

2 celery sticks, trimmed and chopped

225g (8oz) finely shredded fresh spinach, or 100g (3½oz) frozen, thawed and drained

75g (3oz) pine kernels

the grated rind and juice of 1 unwaxed lemon

175g (6oz) fresh white breadcrumbs

1 medium egg, beaten

Heat the oil in a pan and gently fry the onion, garlic, carrot and celery for 5 minutes, until softened. Remove the pan from the heat and stir in the spinach, pine kernels, lemon rind and juice, breadcrumbs and egg. Season to taste, and mix until the stuffing has a stiff consistency.

Stuff half the mixture into the neck cavity of the turkey, then fold over the neck flap and secure it. You can either do this with fine twine and a needle or with skewers.

Roll the remaining stuffing into small balls and place them round the turkey for the last 20 minutes of its cooking time.

Bread Sauce

Duchy Originals milk is sweeter and richer than average and makes very good bread sauce. Nick even likes to eat it cold. Bread sauce plays an important lubricating role in a traditional Christmas dinner.

1 medium onion, studded with 4 cloves

500ml (18fl oz) Duchy Originals or other organic whole milk

100g (3½oz) fresh white breadcrumbs

freshly grated nutmeg

salt and white pepper

50ml (2fl oz) double cream

a blob of butter

Simmer the onion in the milk for 20 minutes, stirring occasionally. Take care not to let the pan boil over.

Remove the onion, pour in the breadcrumbs and stir until the mixture is thickened.

Grate in a little nutmeg, season with salt and pepper and add the double cream and butter.

Heat to boiling point, stirring continuously, and serve immediately.

Venison Saddle Eye Fillet with Port

Serves 2 • Saddle eye is the venison equivalent of fillet steak. It is a tasty and succulent cut which doesn't appreciate being overcooked, so if you like your meat well done, you might be better off with a regular steak. To source the venison, ring round some quality butchers, type 'venison saddle eye' into a search engine or try your local farmers' market.

a small saddle eye fillet of venison (250-300g/9-10½oz)

olive oil

2 teaspoons chopped fresh thyme

salt and pepper

150ml (¼ pint) port

150ml (¼ pint) fresh chicken stock

a bay leaf

Smear the venison in olive oil, salt, pepper and thyme. Fry the fillet over gentle heat for 10 minutes in a dry non-stick pan, turning occasionally so that it cooks evenly. To check how cooked it is, take a peek inside by inserting a sharp knife.

Take the venison out of the pan and leave it to rest next to the stove. Pour the port, chicken stock and bay leaf into the pan you cooked the venison in and rapidly reduce over moderate heat until the volume has decreased by at least two-thirds.

Slice the venison into medallions and serve with the port jus, sautéed potatoes and spinach.

Turkey and Bacon Soup

Serves 4 • This is a splendid way to deal with the remnants of the Christmas turkey. Bits of meat that might not be terribly appetising in themselves come into their own in a good soup.

1 turkey carcass, all meat removed, chopped and reserved

1 onion, roughly chopped

½ leek, washed and roughly sliced

1 carrot, peeled and roughly sliced

1 medium turnip, chopped

6 rashers of Duchy Originals streaky bacon, sliced

a small piece of butter

½ swede, chopped

½ celeriac, chopped

2 medium potatoes, roughly diced

1 teaspoon chopped fresh thyme

4 sage leaves

100ml (3½fl oz) double cream

salt and freshly ground pepper

a handful of flat leaf parsley, roughly chopped

Break up the turkey carcass, place in a large saucepan and just cover with water. Add any vegetables and gravy left over from Christmas lunch and simmer for a couple of hours to make a rich and delicious stock.

Reserve the stock and throw away the bones and vegetable solids. You need just over a litre (1¾ pints) of stock for this soup, so if you have any left over, store it in the fridge for a couple of days or freeze it.

Fry the onion, leek, carrot, turnip and bacon in the butter over moderate heat for about 10 minutes, stirring frequently.

Add the stock, swede, celeriac, potatoes, thyme and sage and simmer for 30-40 minutes. Top up with stock if the soup seems a little thick.

Towards the end, add the turkey meat, double cream, salt and pepper and finally the parsley.

Serve immediately with hunks of crusty bread.

Rolled Pork Loin with a Christmas Fruit and Cognac Stuffing

Serves 6 • This stunning yet simple recipe uses what is known as pork middle, consisting of belly and loin together. You need the meat to be in one piece because you are going to stuff it, roll it and tie it up. When you order your pork, ask for a boned section of belly and loin in one piece from a middle weighing about 2 kg (4lb 8oz). Ask your butcher to score the skin.

The fat from the pork belly gives this dish a tender juiciness. You will end up with a mountain of crispy pork, complemented by a luxurious, fruity stuffing. This recipe works best if you lay the pork on a rack above a tray. This way, it will crisp up all over. You will also need some string (make sure you use string that won't melt in the oven).

1 pork middle

fine sea salt and black pepper

dried rosemary and sage

THE STUFFING

1 small onion, finely diced

½ tablespoon butter

100g (3½oz) minced pork

25g (1oz) chopped dates

25g (1oz) chopped cranberries

100g (3½oz) chopped dried apricots

60g (2½oz) breadcrumbs made from fresh white bread (pulse in the food processor)

40ml (1½fl oz) cognac

zest from 1 orange

1 Bramley apple, diced quite small

Lay the pork middle skin side up on a large plate or tray, and cover with a thin layer of fine sea salt. Rub the salt deep into the cracks. After 2 hours, wash the salt off thoroughly and pat the meat dry.

To make the stuffing, fry the onion in the butter for 5 minutes, stirring frequently. Mix all the ingredients together in a large bowl and leave to rest in the fridge for an hour or two.

Preheat the oven to 240°C/475°F/gas mark 9.

Turn the meat over so the skin side is on the kitchen surface. Mould the stuffing into a sausage and press it into the nook between the eye of the loin and the belly section. Roll the meat up tightly and tie it with string in at least 4 places, with the knots at the bottom.

Splash a bit of olive oil into a bowl and add a teaspoon each of dried sage and dried rosemary, plus some salt and pepper. Rub this mixture all over the outside of the pork with your fingers.

Roast the meat for 20 minutes, then turn down the heat to 180°C/350°F/gas mark 4 and cook on for a further 1 hour and 40 minutes.

Serve with roast potatoes, red cabbage, Duchy chipolatas and Brussels sprouts mixed with bacon lardons.

Stilton Sandwich with Cranberry

Serves 1 • This sandwich contrasts the creamy pungency of stilton with sweet cranberry sauce. Throw in a few walnuts and you have a feast. You may want to have a glass of port while you indulge.

Use any bread of your choice, but as we may have mentioned, the Duchy Originals loaves are rather good!

2 thick slices of bread

unsalted butter

a large spoonful of cranberry sauce

a couple of chunky slices of Duchy Originals stilton

4 walnut halves, broken

4 cherry tomatoes, cut in half

a little scrunched fistful of baby spinach leaves

salt and pepper

Spread both slices of the bread with the butter and then the cranberry sauce.

Lay the stilton on one of the slices and sprinkle the walnut halves and cherry tomatoes on top, adding a little seasoning if you like. Top with the spinach, cover with the other slice of bread and cut diagonally.

Christmas Leftover Sandwich with Turkey, Cheddar and Duchy Originals Honey Mustard

Makes 1 sandwich • Nick spends half his life designing sandwiches, so he prides himself on knowing what makes a good one. The best sandwiches are piled high, filled right to the edges and bursting with colours and textures.

You can use either fresh or toasted bread for this sandwich, and we'd advise you to use Duchy Originals sunflower seed and honey bread.

2 thick slices of Duchy Originals sunflower seed and honey bread

salt and plenty of black pepper

unsalted butter or mayonnaise

1 teaspoon Duchy Originals wholegrain mustard with honey

2 generous slices of turkey breast

enough thick slices of mature cheddar to cover the turkey

4 slices of a medium tomato

a small handful of mixed leaves

Lay the 2 slices of bread out on your kitchen surface and season them with salt and pepper.

Spread both slices with butter or mayonnaise, then the honey mustard. Lay the turkey breast on one slice, followed by the cheddar, tomato and mixed leaves. Don't put the tomato slices on top: if the salt touches them, it will draw out the juices and make the sandwich soggy.

Cover the sandwich with the other slice of bread and cut diagonally from corner to corner with a sharp knife.

MINCEMEAT

In medieval times, mincemeat really did contain minced meat, eked out with dried fruits and spices, but by the nineteenth century the only animal product in traditional Christmas mince pies was suet. Today, even that tends to be vegetarian, as it is in the Duchy Originals version.

Alan Davis is primarily a bread-maker, but he also produces some of the finest mincemeat in the country. He left his job with British Telecom in 1994, and, because he was dissatisfied with the quality of bread then available in Britain, promptly set up a bakery in his garage in partnership with a friend from Shipton Mill. He founded The Authentic Bread Company the following year, and in 1999 the firm moved to its current premises in a converted sows' shed in the Forest of Dean.

Alan is a big, bearded man with an infectious love of good food. He has been making mincemeat for Duchy Originals since 2003, during which time the quantity produced has risen exponentially from four tonnes to thirty five. In 2004, he had to work two 18-hour shifts followed by one of 24 hours to fulfil his quota of 11,000 mince pies.

The mincemeat is made in 200kg (440lb) batches. The first thing we notice in the mixing room is a powerful aroma of apples. It emanates from organic Bramleys, which are currently being hand-cored in large numbers. They are grown in nearby Herefordshire, and arrive at the Authentic Bread Company towards the end of August. The other ingredients, in no particular order, are clear, uncaramelised cognac, vegetarian suet, raisins, currants, sultanas, lemon and orange zest and juice, sunflower oil, mixed spice, cane sugar and flaked almonds. As they are slowly mixed together, we experience a powerful urge to dive into the vat.

Above Organic Bramley apples. Below The cores are removed by hand. Then all the ingredients are mixed together, including organic cane sugar, cognac and lemon zest. Bottom, far right Alan Davis presiding over the mixing machine.

Crumble Mince Slices

Makes 16–20 squares or bars • With regular mince pies now appearing in the shops as early as August, these crumble slices come as a welcome alternative by the time we reach December. They are cooked in one mass in a baking tray and sliced into squares or bars afterwards, rather like flapjacks.

You can buy good-quality mincemeat in the shops, but it is more satisfying to make it yourself. The recipe below will produce five or six jars worth. It is hardly worth making in smaller quantities, and any excess you may have will make excellent seasonal gifts for friends or relatives. You should prepare the mincemeat several weeks in advance to give it time to mature.

THE MINCEMEAT

4 medium Bramley apples, cored and finely diced (add a little lemon juice to prevent browning)

2 lemons, zested and squeezed

2 oranges, zested and squeezed

400g (14oz) raisins

400g (14oz) currants

200g (7oz) dried cranberries

250g (9oz) suet (vegetarian if you prefer)

500g (18oz) soft brown sugar

100g (3½oz) candied orange peel finely chopped

100g (3½oz) chopped almonds

½ teaspoon ground cinnamon

½ teaspoon ground ginger

¼ nutmeg, grated

125ml (4fl oz) brandy

100ml (3½fl oz) Grand Marnier or other orange liqueur

THE CRUMBLE

300g (10½oz) Duchy Originals shortbread biscuits, crushed in the food processor or with a pestle and mortar

40g (1½oz) unsalted butter

THE PASTRY

200g (7oz) plain flour

75g (3oz) butter

50g (2oz) icing sugar

1½ large eggs (to divide an egg in half, lightly whip and divide into 2 portions)

a couple of drops of vanilla essence

To make the mincemeat, combine all the ingredients except the alcohol in a large mixing bowl.

Transfer to a greased baking dish with a lid, cover and leave for an hour or two while the flavours meld.

Preheat the oven to 120°C/250°F/gas mark ½ and bake for 3 or 4 hours.

Leave the mincemeat to cool, but stir it from time to time to prevent the fat from coagulating into one big lump.

When the mincemeat is cool, stir in the alcohol and immediately pot it up in sterile jars. It will keep for at least a year if you store the jars in a cool dark place without opening them.

To make the crumble, simply mix the crushed biscuits and butter in a bowl until you can't see the butter anymore.

To make the pastry, rub the flour, butter and icing sugar together in a large bowl with the tips of your fingers. Do this for 5 minutes or so. Then stir in the eggs and vanilla essence with a spoon.

Turn the pastry out onto the work surface and lightly knead. Mould it into a ball and store in the fridge until needed.

Now you are ready to put everything together. Preheat the oven to 180°C/350°F/gas mark 4. In the meantime roll the pastry into a rectangle and place on a large greased baking sheet. Gently spread a layer of mincemeat about 1½–2cm (¾in) deep onto the rolled pastry, and sprinkle with the crumble. Bake for 30–35 minutes until golden brown. Cut into slices while still warm, but don't remove them from the tray until they have cooled or they may fall apart.

Date and Walnut Cake

Makes one large cake • This cake is based on a recipe for Sodbury Cake, as in the market town of Chipping Sodbury in Gloucestershire, and was well-known to be a favourite of the late Queen Mother. We have tinkered with the recipe enough to make the cake only vaguely reminiscent of the original, but it is extremely good nonetheless.

For this recipe, you will need a large loaf tin that has been greased with butter and lined with greaseproof paper.

100g (3½oz) whole almonds

100g (3½oz) whole pecans

100ml (3½fl oz) maple syrup

50g (2oz) tamarind pulp

200g (7oz) unsalted butter, at room temperature

150g (5½oz) soft dark brown sugar

50g (2oz) caster sugar

2 large eggs

100g (3½oz) broken walnut pieces

200g (7oz) dates, unstoned and chopped

½ teaspoon cinnamon

¼ of a grated whole nutmeg

150g (5½oz) plain flour

2 teaspoons baking powder

Preheat the oven to 180ºC/350ºF/gas mark 4.

Bake the almonds and pecans in the oven for 6 minutes, remove, then turn the heat down to 160ºC/325ºF/just under gas mark 3, pending the arrival of the prepared cake.

Blend the almonds and pecans to the consistency of rough flour and place them in a little bowl.

Heat the maple syrup in a saucepan with the tamarind pulp. As soon as the contents come to the boil, remove from the heat and mash them with a fork to release the tamarind pulp from the fibres and seeds. Push the resulting liquid through a sieve with a spoon and discard the fibrous mass left behind.

Cream together the butter, brown sugar and caster sugar until pale and fluffy. You can use a whisk, mixer or food processor.

Lightly whip the eggs and gradually incorporate them into the butter and sugar mix, whipping constantly.

Add the tamarind, ground almonds, pecans, walnut pieces, dates, cinnamon and nutmeg, and sift in the baking powder and flour. Mix thoroughly.

Spoon the mixture into the loaf tin and bake for 1 hour.

Turn the cake out onto a wire rack and leave it to cool. It will keep for at least a week in an airtight container.

CHRISTMAS PUDDING

As with medieval mince pies, the ancestor of the Christmas Pudding contained minced meat. Prior to the invention of the pudding cloth, it was a sloppy affair, eaten in Winter but with no particular association with Christmas. It was typically served at the beginning of the meal rather than at the end, and incorporated root vegetables and dried fruits. Plums, in the form of prunes, were first added in the sixteenth century, and by 1670 'Plum Pottage' was an integral part of Christmas dinner. The recipe for what we now regard as traditional Christmas Pudding was formalised in the nineteenth century.

The award-winning Duchy Originals version is based on an old recipe and has a pronounced Victorian feel. It is light and fruity with a moist crumbly texture. The main ingredients are apples, breadcrumbs, crystallised ginger, grated carrot (a legacy of the original root vegetable component), walnuts, spices, sweet almonds, English ale, cognac and 'Empire fruits with new laid egg'.

Tradition dictates that Christmas Pudding should be aflame with burning alcohol when it is brought to table. The key to a successful conflagration is to warm the alcohol, preferably brandy, in a pan before pouring it over the pudding and igniting it. It is customary to serve Christmas Pudding with Brandy Butter (see recipe on page 205), but cream, custard and ice cream are also excellent accompaniments. Another tradition is to bury a silver sixpence or other trinket somewhere in the pudding and let fate decide which diner is to be the lucky recipient.

Christmas Pudding Fritters

Serves 4 • Christmas Pudding is one of the world's more filling dishes, especially when you have just gorged yourself on turkey or goose, and there always seems to be some left over. The perennial problem of what to do with it is easily solved by these tasty fritters.

200-300g (7-10½oz) leftover Duchy Originals christmas pudding

100g (3½oz) flour

25g (1oz) icing sugar

125ml (4fl oz) white wine

25ml (1fl oz) Grand Marnier

vegetable oil for deep frying

Break up the Christmas pudding and roll the pieces into balls.

Sift the flour and icing sugar into a bowl, then whisk in the white wine and Grand Marnier until you have a smooth batter.

Heat the oil in a wok until a little batter thrown in fizzes up to the surface.

Dip the balls into the batter with a spoon, then slide them in to the oil.

Cook the fritters in small batches for 3 or 4 minutes until golden brown, then remove them from the oil with a slotted spoon.

Serve with brandy butter (see page 205).

Christmas Plum Cake

Makes one cake • Many recipes for Plum Cake in cookery books are strikingly plum-free, and those that are not usually contain very few of them. This nutless, marzipanless version does its best to rectify the situation by incorporating almost a pound of prunes (dried plums), as well as several other fruits.

You could ice this cake or cover it in nuts if you wanted to, but we advise you to eat it plain, un-aged and covered in brandy.

200g (7oz) cherries preserved in kirsch

100ml (3½fl oz) of the kirsch syrup

200g (7oz) seedless raisins

400g (14oz) chopped pitted prunes (prunes from Agen in France are very juicy and tasty)

200g (7oz) soft dried figs, chopped

zest of an orange

zest of a lemon

1 tablespoon brandy

175g (6oz) plain flour

½ teaspoon cinnamon powder

½ teaspoon grated nutmeg

1 heaped teaspoon baking powder

½ teaspoon salt

225g (8oz) unsalted butter, at room temperature

1 tablespoon dark muscovado sugar

225g (8oz) light muscovado or soft brown sugar

4 large eggs, lightly whipped
50g (2oz) ground almonds

1 tablespoon treacle

First, place the cherries, kirsch, raisins, prunes, figs, zest and brandy in a large bowl. Stir the mixture every 20 minutes or so, and within 2 hours, all the alcohol will have been soaked up, and the fruits will have plumped up delightfully.

Preheat the oven to 140ºC/275ºF/gas mark 1.

Grease a cake tin with a removable base. (Ours is 24cm/10in across and 8cm/3in deep). To do this wipe all the inside surfaces with a thin layer of butter using the butter wrapper, then sprinkle with a thin layer of flour, shaking off any excess.

Sift the flour into a bowl along with the spices, baking powder and salt and reserve.

Cream the butter and the dark and light muscovado sugars together in a large bowl with a spoon for a few minutes until the mixture pales up and becomes a bit fluffier. It helps if the butter is warm but not melted.

Scrape the mixture off the spoon and pick up a whisk. Slowly whisk in the eggs, bit by bit, so that it doesn't curdle (if it does, just add a little of the flour.)

Fold in the flour along with the ground almonds. Then thoroughly mix in the treacle and fruit and pour into the cake tin.

Loosely wrap the cake with greaseproof paper and bake for 3 hours or so. To check whether the cake is done, remove it after the specified period and insert a wooden toothpick into the middle. If the mix adheres to the stick, leave the cake in the oven for a little longer.

If you can persuade yourself not to eat this cake immediately, you can store it in a tin for several months. If you do this, pour a liberal quantity of brandy over it before storage to preserve it.

CHOCOLATE

Christmas wouldn't be Christmas without chocolates, and Duchy Originals offers several tempting options in this department. The range encompasses Luxury Chocolate Truffles, made from both dark and milk chocolate and indulgently filled with Marc de Champagne, ginger, cognac and other delicacies, a Luxury Chocolate Assortment which includes truffles, fruit and nut clusters and chocolates filled with ganache, Chocolate Thins in both milk and dark varieties, and Orange Peel and Ginger Stems encased in dark chocolate. The company also makes Easter Eggs stamped with the Duchy crest, but that is another story.

The Duchy chocolates are made with a mixture of organic cocoa beans sourced from Brazil and the Dominican Republic. Duchy Originals will soon also source cocoa beans from a co-operative of 26 farmers in Guyana. The partnership began when Prince Charles visited the country in 2000 and learned that the cocoa industry, which had once been a cornerstone of the Guyanan economy, had been dormant for thirty years. The Prince suggested to the President that he might like to revive cocoa production on the old plantations to provide top-quality chocolate for his organic food business. As a result, and with the help of the National Agricultural Research Institute, the above mentioned co-operative was established.

THE MOLTEN CENTRE

125g (4½oz) dark chocolate
(70 per cent cocoa solids)

15g (¾oz) butter

50ml (2fl oz) double cream

25g (1oz) caster sugar

THE PUDDING

200g (7oz) dark chocolate
(70 per cent cocoa solids)

100g (3½oz) unsalted butter,
at room temperature

100g (3½oz) caster sugar

6 eggs divided into yolks and
whites

100g (3½oz) plain flour

40g (1½oz) cornflour

1½ teaspoons baking powder

Molten Chocolate Pudding

This pudding can be likened to a volcano. When you cut into it, molten chocolate 'lava' will erupt from the centre. It is therefore spectacular as well as delicious.

You will need a medium-sized pudding bowl with a capacity of 1.5-1.8 litres (2½-3 pints) or small individual ramekins, and a lidded saucepan into which it or they will fit. The saucepan in turn needs to be able to fit into the oven.

First make the molten centre. Melt all the ingredients in a pan over very low heat. As soon as the last chunk of chocolate has melted, pour the contents of the pan into a small bowl, cover it and leave it to set in the freezer for approximately 20 minutes until firm.

To make the pudding, first heat the oven to 180°C/350°F/gas mark 4.

Grease the bowl with a little butter smeared on its wrapper, wiping around until there is a thin layer all around the inside. Sift in a little flour and shake the bowl around until the butter is covered with a dusting of flour. This will allow the pudding to rise smoothly.

Slowly melt the pudding chocolate in a small bowl over hot water or in a microwave. Cream the butter and sugar in a large bowl with a wooden spoon for a minute or two until pale and fluffy. Then take a whisk and whisk in the egg yolks one by one.

Whip the egg whites into soft peaks and reserve.

Add the flour, cornflour and baking powder to the butter/sugar/egg mix and stir them in with a wooden spoon.

Next, fold in the melted chocolate, then the egg whites. Start with just a small proportion of the whites, then when the mixture has loosened up fold in the rest until incorporated.

Pour a third of the mix into the pudding bowl, then retrieve the chocolate from the freezer and lay the set 'plug' on top. Finally, add the rest of the pudding mix. Cover the bowl with greaseproof paper and tin foil.

Place the pudding in its bowl in the saucepan and carefully pour in water until it comes halfway up the bowl. Take care not to pour any water into the pudding itself.

Put the lid on the saucepan and bring to the boil on the stove top. As soon as the contents begin to bubble, place the saucepan in the oven, and leave it there for 1 hour. If you are making small puddings, bake for 30 minutes. You can also cook the puddings in a steamer.

Take the saucepan out of the oven and remove the lid. Carefully extract the pudding from the bowl and leave it to rest for 15 minutes before serving.

Serve with double cream or vanilla ice cream. To continue the volcano analogy, either works wonderfully as the 'snow'.

Chocolate Mousse, made with
Duchy Originals Tangerine Thins

Serves 4 • This recipe is quick and simple, and the results are highly impressive. You will need four ramekins. Like all the best mousses, this one is light and fluffy, characteristics likely to be welcomed by anyone who has overindulged.

14 Duchy Originals chocolate tangerine thins

a small knob of butter (about a heaped teaspoon)

the whites of 2 large eggs

50g (2oz) caster sugar

100ml (3½fl oz) double cream

Melt the tangerine thins with the butter in a small bowl over hot water.

Whisk the egg whites and caster sugar until soft peaks form. When you pull out the whisk it should leave soft peaks in its wake.

Transfer the egg whites into another bowl, using a spatula.

Pour the cream into the same bowl you used to whisk the egg whites (there's no need to wash it first) and whisk until thick but not completely firm. Then transfer the cream to the bowl containing the whipped egg whites.

Pour most of the chocolate into the cream and whipped egg whites, leaving a couple of teaspoons worth at the bottom. Fold all the ingredients together until smooth.

Spoon the mousse into 4 ramekins and smooth it down. Then swirl threads of the remaining melted chocolate on top using a teaspoon.

Leave the mousses to set in the fridge for at least an hour before serving. You can make them the day before eating them if you wish, but make sure you cover them while they are in the fridge.

Fluffy Orange Brownies

Makes about 15 brownies • When Johnny was a teenager, he went to a fast-food restaurant in Washington DC where he was presented with a 36-part questionnaire solely about the chocolate brownies. The only pressing question about these ones is 'should I have another one?' They are made with Duchy chocolate thins and chocolate coated orange peel, are flour and gluten free and quite delicious.

You will need a shallow baking tray around 20 x 30cm (8 x 12in).

175g whole almonds, baked for 10 minutes at 180°C/350°F/gas mark 4

20 Duchy Originals chocolate thins (leaving around 7 in the packet for you)

25g (1oz) unsalted butter

2 large eggs

80g (3oz) caster sugar

100g (3½oz) Duchy Originals chocolate coated orange peel (two-thirds of a packet)

Preheat the oven to 180°C/350°F/gas mark 4.

Rub the baking tray with butter and line it with greaseproof paper.

Blend the almonds in the food processor until they are ground down as fine as they will go.

Melt the chocolate thins with the butter in a small bowl over another filled with hot water.

Beat the eggs and the sugar with an electric mixer on high speed for 3-5 minutes until the mixture keeps its shape and only gradually subsides.

Empty the melted chocolate into the egg mixture along with the almonds and chocolate orange peel. Gently fold them in with a spatula.

Spread the mixture evenly onto the baking tray and bake for 15 minutes.

Let the brownie mass cool in the tray, then lift it out and cut it into portions.

Vanilla ice cream is an excellent accompaniment.

Basic Recipes

The following recipes have been placed at the back of the book either because they are 'staples' used in several of our recipes, or in the case of Brandy Butter, because there was simply not enough space to fit it in the Christmas section.

Old English pastry

250g (9oz) flour

½ teaspoon salt

75g (3oz) suet

75g (3oz) butter

cold water

Sift the flour into a large bowl, then add the salt.

Add the suet and butter and rub in using the tips of your fingers. Take your time.

Stick your hand in the mixture and slowly pour in water, squeezing and manipulating until you have a stiff dough.

Turn the dough out on to the work surface and knead it with the heel of your hand for a minute or two. Roll it into a sausage, wrap them in cling film and store in the fridge until needed.

Cheese pastry

120g (4½oz) plain flour

60g (2½oz) butter

25g (1oz) grated cheddar

a pinch of salt

a little grated nutmeg

2 large egg yolks

half the white from 1 large egg

First sift the flour onto your work surface. Then cut the butter into small cubes and place them on top of the flour together with the cheese, salt and nutmeg. Rub the ingredients together with the tips of your fingers until all the lumps of butter and cheese have melted into the mix.

Make a well in the centre and add the 2 yolks and egg white. Work the egg in with your fingers. This is messy but enjoyable; you can use a plastic scraper to remove the pastry from your hands.

Gather the pastry into a ball and work it with the heel of your hand for 30 seconds. Use the pastry itself to mop up all the loose bits on the surface because it's stickier than anything else.

Work the pastry again for a minute, then shape it into a ball, wrap in cling film and store in the fridge until needed.

Lamb stock

(MAKES ABOUT 1 LITRE/
1¾ PINTS)

1kg (2¼lb) lamb bones and trimmings

2 medium carrots, washed and trimmed

2 sticks of celery

1 medium onion

2 garlic cloves

a sprig each of rosemary and thyme

Preheat the oven to 200ºC/400ºF/gas mark 6 and bake all the stock ingredients apart from the rosemary and thyme for 1 hour.

After roasting, transfer the ingredients to a saucepan along with the herbs. Add enough water to just cover the contents, and simmer for at least 2 hours (preferably 4). Strain off the stock and discard the solids.

If you make this stock in advance, store it in the fridge and peel off the solid fat before use. You can freeze any excess. If you are using the stock immediately, you will need to skim the fat that rises to the surface during simmering with a ladle.

Brandy butter

150g (5½oz) unsalted butter, room temperature. The warmer it is (without being melted) the better

150g (5½oz) soft brown sugar

4 tablespoons brandy, or Grand Marnier or spiced rum if you feel experimental

Serves everyone around the average Christmas table — about 6 people.
There is little to be said for buying brandy butter. It only has three ingredients and is terribly easy to make. Your Christmas Pudding and mince pies won't be the same without it.

Whisk up the butter and sugar until pale, soft and creamy.
Add the brandy by degrees, beating well until it is all incorporated. Taste the brandy butter and add a little more alcohol if you deem it necessary. Place in the fridge until needed. You can make your brandy butter well in advance; it will keep in the fridge for weeks.

Index